Spiritual Warfare

Joining Jesus in Conquering Evil

DAVID FEDDES

Christian Leaders Press

Monee, Illinois

christianleadersinstitute.org

We are more than conquerors
through him who loved us.

CONTENTS

CONTENTS

Part One

Christ the Commander:
Serving Under General Jesus

May God arise, may his enemies be scattered, may his foes flee before him.
(Psalm 68:1)

Do not suppose that I have come to bring peace to the earth. I did not come to bring peace, but a sword.   (Matthew 10:34)

I saw heaven standing open and there before me was a white horse, whose rider is called Faithful and True. With justice he judges and makes war.   (Revelation 19:11)

Be strong in the Lord and in his mighty power.   (Ephesians 6:10)

Chapter One

Jesus the Troublemaker

I did not come to bring peace, but a sword. (Matthew 10:34)

Jesus is the world's greatest troublemaker. He disturbs the peace and causes fights. Jesus arouses conflict and turns family members against each other. Some people even end up dying because of Jesus. Here's what Jesus himself says:

> Do not suppose that I have come to bring peace to the earth. I did not come to bring peace, but a sword. For I have come to turn a man against his father, a daughter against her mother, a daughter-in-law against her mother-in-law—a man's enemies will be the members of his own household.
>
> Anyone who loves his father or mother more than me is not worthy of me; anyone who loves his son or daughter more than me is not worthy of me; and anyone who does not take his cross and follow me is not worthy of me. Whoever finds his life will lose it, and whoever loses his life for my sake will find it (Matthew 10:34-39).

We might expect such words from an anti-family religious nut or from the leader of a wacko suicide cult. But the troublemaker who says these things is Jesus.

Those aren't the first words most preachers quote when calling people to Jesus. Those of us who are preachers usually figure that if we want to "sell" people on Jesus, we'd better advertise him as a problem solver, not a troublemaker. We'd better picture Jesus as a source of peace in troubled times, not as a cause of conflict. We'd better present him as a therapist for troubled families, not as someone who divides families. We speak of him as the one who can save your life, not as the one who makes you lose your life. We say things like, "If you want peace in this troubled world, come to Jesus. If you want help with family problems, come to Jesus. If you want your life to be all it can be, come to Jesus."

Combat Commander

"Be all that you can be"—that's an old slogan of army recruiters, and sometimes we preachers sound like those recruiters. Recruiters for the military know that strife is the army's job. If your commanding officer orders you into combat, you must be willing to go wherever he commands. You must be willing to abandon father and mother, wife and children, brothers and sisters, even your own life. You must obey your commanding officer, no matter what. Army recruiters know this—but do the advertisements show a lonely soldier longing for people back home, or family members who are sad and angry at their loved one for leaving, or horrifying scenes of combat and death? No, recruiters produce ads that look exciting and inviting.

We preachers do something similar. We try to enlist people in Jesus' army by telling them all the advantages and none of the troubles. For some reason, though, Jesus himself doesn't stick to such positive advertising. Yes, he promises great things, but he also speaks about strife and division, family problems, and loss of life—the sort of troubles that any combat commander causes. What if we preachers, in our eagerness to recruit people for Jesus, aren't telling the whole truth about him?

You may find it hard to think of Jesus as a troublemaker. With so many preachers talking about a nice, helpful

Jesus whose only goal is to help us be all that we can be, it's hard to see why anyone would want to crucify him. But people who met the real Jesus had no problem at all seeing him as a troublemaker. They saw him as strange, even dangerous. "Even his own brothers did not believe in him" (John 7:5). His family once tried to stop him from teaching and wanted to take him home, because they thought he was out of his mind (Mark 3:21). Some religious leaders concluded that Jesus was possessed by the prince of demons (Mark 3:22). Some of the common people also thought he was demon-possessed (John 7:20). If you doubt that people saw Jesus as a threat and a troublemaker, why do you think they killed him? Maybe you've imagined Jesus as helpful and harmless. But what if he's really the fighter and troublemaker he claims to be? What then? Will you follow him?

It may sound foolish, even crazy, to follow Jesus if he's a troublemaker. He says, "I did not come to bring peace, but a sword... a man's enemies will be the members of his own household." What does Jesus mean?

Let's be clear about one thing right away: Jesus doesn't cause trouble just for the sake of trouble. He comes as God to reclaim a world which has turned against God, and that means a fight. Whenever a ruler starts to reclaim territories and people who have turned against him, it's impossible to avoid strife. Jesus came into this world to reclaim it for God and to rescue it from enemy occupation by Satan and his demons. Jesus' coming arouses resistance from the realm of demons. Jesus' coming divides people between those who continue to side with sinful powers and those who side with Jesus. So if you enlist in Jesus' army and follow him, you had better be ready for conflict.

Worthy of Complete Loyalty

Your loyalty to Jesus is bound to create problems with people around you, even with family members. Jesus calls for absolute, undivided loyalty. We must follow him even if it causes trouble, not just if he makes our family life easier. We must be willing to alienate ourselves from people we love in order to follow Jesus.

This may sound troubling at first, but think about it. Suppose you decide to follow Jesus on the grounds that he might help you to succeed in your family life or in your business. You don't love Jesus or care about him, but you figure he can help you out in some things that really matter to you. Well, Jesus isn't interested in that kind of a relationship. He wants you to love him, not use him.

What would you think of someone who pretended to be your friend just to get what he wants from you? How eager would you be to marry someone who is only interested in your money? Not very appealing, is it? So why should the Son of God put up with being used by people who don't love him? Don't come to Jesus for what he can do for your family life or your business. Come to Jesus simply because you love him more than anyone and because he deserves your highest loyalty.

If Jesus were just one more religious nut who causes strife and disrupts families and demands complete loyalty, it would be crazy to follow him. But Jesus isn't just some crazy guy who thinks he's God; Jesus *is* God. As God he is supremely worthy of our love, since his divine love is far greater than that of any person we know. And as God he is also supremely worthy of the absolute, unconditional obedience that a soldier owes to his supreme commander. No matter what trouble it might cause in your other relationships, love and absolute obedience to Jesus come first. That's the only fitting response to who he is as God.

It's also the only realistic response. You might as well know what you're getting into if you're thinking about following Jesus. If an easy, trouble-free life is what you're after, then Jesus the troublemaker isn't for you. If you like your relationships just the way they are, and you're unwilling for any of that to change, then forget about Jesus. He changes everything, and not all of the changes will be pleasant for you, at least not in the short term. Yes, Jesus promises to bring you joy and deliver you from many troubles; but he also warns that you will have troubles that you might not have had if you didn't follow him. Jesus is very honest about that. He wants you to know what you're getting into right up front, with no fine print or deceptive advertising.

Lesser Loves

Jesus wants you to know that as long as you put family ties first, you can't follow him. Your loyalty to Jesus must be unchallenged by any other loyalty. Your love for Jesus must come ahead of all lesser loves. You can't let anyone else get in the way of your relationship to Jesus. What does this look like in everyday life? Here are some examples.

Suppose you come from a family that doesn't follow Jesus. You identify with your mother and father, your brothers and sisters, and with your family's way of life. Perhaps you even have a bit of ritual or religion in your family, but not a living faith in Jesus. If that's the case, you can't follow Christ unless you turn away from what your family members are like and what they expect you to be like. That's not easy. It's terribly hard to admit to yourself that Jesus is right and your family is wrong. To you it may feel like you're hating and rejecting your family, and it may feel that way to them too. In some societies, family members actually try to kill their relatives who leave their family's religion to follow Jesus. And even if your family doesn't do that, you may sense that your family isn't comfortable around you once you've become a Christian. You feel strong pressure from them to return to the way you were. Only by rejecting your family's wishes can you follow the way of Jesus. Loyalty to Jesus comes first.

Another kind of relationship where Jesus causes trouble is romance. Once you become a Christian, Jesus doesn't permit you to marry someone who doesn't also belong to him. You shouldn't even have a dating relationship with such a person. Samson was a mighty man, but he became attached to the ungodly woman Delilah, and she was his downfall. Solomon was a brilliant king, but he married women who worshipped other gods, and they turned his heart away from the Lord. So unless you're stronger than Samson and smarter than Solomon, don't violate your relationship with God by pursuing romantic relationships with non-Christians. Love for Jesus must come ahead of all lesser loves.

Olivia Langdon was raised in a Christian home by devout parents, and she claimed to be a Christian herself. One day, she met the brilliant writer Mark Twain. She was charmed by his intelligence and humor. Mark Twain was an open critic of religion, but Olivia thought she could marry him and then help him become a Christian.

At first, it seemed to be working. As one biographer puts it, Twain's "natural kindness of heart, and especially his love for his wife, inclined him toward the teachings and customs of her Christian faith ... It took very little persuasion on his wife's part to establish family prayers in their home, grace before meals, and the morning reading of the Bible chapter."

As time passed, however, Twain got tired of pretending. He told Olivia, "Livy, you may keep this up if you want to, but I must ask you to excuse me from it. It is making me a hypocrite. I don't believe in the Bible; it contradicts my reason. I can't sit here and listen to it, letting you believe that I regard it, as you do, in the light of the Gospel, the Word of God." Olivia had failed to persuade her husband to become a Christian.

But the worst was yet to come. Some years later, Olivia told her sister that she no longer believed in a personal God who cared for every human soul. Then came a time when Olivia felt crushed by the death of a loved one. Twain told her, "Livy, if it comforts you to lean on your Christian faith, do so."

She replied, "I can't. I haven't any."

That story has been repeated many times. People think they can marry a non-Christian and continue to follow Jesus, but already in making that choice, they have put loyalty to their loved one ahead of loyalty to God. All too often they either end up abandoning faith in God, or else living at odds with their spouse. That's why the Bible says, "Do not be yoked together with unbelievers...What does a believer have in common with an unbeliever?" (2 Corinthians 6:14-15). If you're a Christian dating a non-Christian, end the relationship. Follow Christ.

But what if this warning has come too late for you? What if you're already married to someone who doesn't follow Jesus? In that case, you may have a hard road ahead of you. But you can still follow Jesus if he moves you to love him more than you love your husband or wife. Ask Jesus to forgive what you've done. Commit yourself to following the way of Christ. Live by the Bible's teachings. Worship each week with other Christians. If your husband or wife becomes upset about any of this, don't let it stop you. You can't compromise your commitment to Christ in order to make your marriage easier. Jesus matters even more than your marriage.

Please don't misunderstand. You shouldn't try to cause trouble with your spouse, and you can't end a marriage the way you can end a dating relationship. You've made those marriage vows, and you must take them seriously. God hates divorce. He doesn't want Christians trying to get rid of unbelieving spouses. Still, the fact remains that if you become a living, active follower of Jesus, you will be different than you were before. If your husband or wife can accept the new you, great! If you keep living as the person

Jesus calls you to be, you may win your spouse over to Christ. But even if your spouse is uncomfortable with your new life in Christ, don't stop following the Lord just to make your marriage more comfortable. You have no choice but to follow Jesus, even if your spouse finds it hateful.

You must love Jesus more than husband or wife, and you must love him more than your sons and daughters too. If loyalty to your children comes before loyalty to Christ, it can distort and destroy your faithfulness to God. How can this happen? Here are a few examples. Your daughter decides to live with a man, and you think, "Maybe marriage isn't the only proper context for sexual intimacy as the Bible claims." Or your son informs you he is gay, and you figure the Bible must be wrong to say that homosexual behavior is sinful. Or some people you love reject Jesus to follow another way, and you can't bear the thought of them going to hell. You become more concerned about them than about God's honor and truth, and you start to wonder if maybe Jesus isn't the only way to eternal life. Your ideas change to suit the behavior of your loved ones. Your love for them eats away at your convictions about God's truth.

Cruel to Be Kind

The sad irony in all this is that if you love other people more than you love Jesus, you're not in a position to help them. You can't accept the plain teaching of the Bible, so you can't help your loved ones to change their ways. You say only what they want to hear rather than what they need to hear. They are so important to you that you can't risk offending them or losing them. And because you can't risk losing them now, you instead allow them to be lost for all eternity. Only when you oppose their behavior for Jesus' sake can you truly love them and help them come to the Lord they need so much. Even if it feels cruel to put loyalty to Jesus ahead of loyalty to loved ones, you must be cruel to be kind.

So far we've seen some examples of what happens when you love unbelieving, sinful family members more than you love Jesus. But what if the people close to you are devout Christians? Well, even then, it can wreck your faith to love them more than you love Jesus. Suppose God takes those people from you. What then?

The Bible tells about Job and his wife. They had a close-knit, God-fearing family, and they were prosperous. Then tragedy struck. Their children were all killed, their wealth vanished, and Job was struck by an illness that caused excruciating pain. How did Job's wife react? She wanted nothing more to do with God. She told her husband, "Are you still holding on to your integrity? Curse God and die!" Job replied, "You are talking like a foolish woman. Shall we accept good from God and not trouble?" (Job 2:9-10)

When God allowed Mrs. Job's children and her prosperity and her husband's health to be taken away, she began to hate God. Why? Because all along she had loved her children and her wealth and her successful husband more than she loved God. Job wasn't like that. Job loved God even more than he loved his wife and children, more than he loved his own life. He grieved his losses and asked many questions, but he refused to stop trusting God. And by loving God more than his children and by rejecting the advice of his own beloved wife, Job held on to God and called his wife back to God as well. In order to have a faith strong enough to survive tragedy, you need a love for Jesus that is greater than your love for anybody else. A half-hearted relationship to Christ can't survive. When your loyalty is tested, you would rather abandon Jesus than lose a relationship with someone you love.

Counting the Cost

When Jesus tells you all this, is he trying to discourage you from following him? No, quite the opposite: he's calling and urging you to follow him. But he wants you to know what you're getting into. Jesus is an honest recruiter. He wants you to count the cost ahead of time. There are great and eternal rewards in following Jesus, but there are also risks and losses. God may give you many blessings, but he may also take away some things and disrupt relationships that are important to you. Do you love him enough to follow him even then? Jesus doesn't want fair-weather friends. He wants disciples who love and follow him, no matter what.

Maybe it sounds like Jesus is demanding too much. But as you count the cost of following him, make sure you also count the cost of not following him. If you try to hold onto your own life on your own terms, you will lose it. You will forever cut yourself off from the Lord and his blessings. That is a terrible price to pay.

Count the cost of following Jesus, count the cost of not following him, and then count one more cost: the cost to Jesus of coming into this world to rescue you from enemy forces and to make you his own. If you think the Lord demands a lot from you, keep in mind that he has given far more than he demands. The Jesus who calls us to give up everything for him is the same Jesus who gave up everything for us. And he had a lot more to give up. Jesus left his place in heaven at his Father's side to become a tiny baby. He gave up his position of power to become a weak human being. And that's not all he gave up. Here on earth, there were times when Jesus had to ignore the human family he loved so much. They wanted him to stop preaching and come home. But Jesus decided: "No matter what my family says, I've got to do what God sent me to do. My real family is anyone who does the will of my Father in heaven" (Mark 3:21, 31-35).

Jesus even laid down his own life, in order to please his Father and to save us. His death was horrible for him, and it pierced his mother's soul. But Jesus loved his heavenly Father even more than he loved his mother and brothers, even more than he loved his own life, and so he took up the cross and laid down his life as his heavenly Father directed him. So yes, Jesus may cause trouble for us, but not nearly as much trouble as he suffered on our behalf. He ignored his own welfare and the wishes of his family in order to carry out God's plan. And in doing so, he opened the way to eternal life for his mother, his brothers, and for everyone else who comes to trust in him.

What's your response to Jesus the troublemaker? Have you enlisted in his army? Do you trust and obey him as your commander? Some troublemakers are bad, but Jesus is one troublemaker you can't live without. You can't live without the troubles he suffered for you. You can't live without him troubling your status quo with his revolutionary gift of new life. You've heard his outrageous demand to love and follow him no matter what. You've also heard his outrageous love and sacrifice for you. Now what? How are you going to respond?

Chapter Two

The Ultimate War Hero

With justice he judges and makes war. (Rev. 19:11)

On June 6, 1944, thousands of soldiers splashed onto the beaches of Normandy, France, amid explosions and a deadly barrage of bullets from German machine guns. D-Day was awful and wonderful: awful because of the terror, pain, and death; wonderful because the forces of freedom triumphed over the forces of oppression.

We should not glorify war or think that killing or dying is glamorous. But neither should we ignore the heroism of those who fought for freedom. The world would be very different if Germany's Nazi regime had not been defeated—if there had been no one smart enough to come up with a strategy, no one brave enough to face ferocious opposition, no one selfless enough to risk being maimed or killed, or no force powerful enough to win the victory. And so, when we think back to the horrors and heroes of D-Day, we honor those who changed history for the better.

War heroes come in different varieties. Some are heroes because of their strategy. General Dwight Eisenhower, for example, was hailed for his role in planning the Normandy landing and directing the allied forces on D-Day. Others are heroes because of their bravery. While all who serve in the armed forces face some danger, those who fought on the front lines and in the deadliest spots are honored as especially heroic. Others are heroes not only because of the risks they faced but because of the price they actually paid. Those who were wounded or captured or tortured or killed hold a unique place in the ranks of war heroes. And then, of course, the heroes include those who survive the battles, overpower the opposition, and parade triumphantly into a city they've liberated, surrounded by the welcoming cheers of grateful residents who have finally been set free from brutal enemy occupation. Different war heroes are special for different reasons: strategy, bravery, sacrifice, or victory.

Who would be the ultimate war hero? We can't really compare. We can't say that a general devising a brilliant strategy back at headquarters is more heroic than a private charging forward through enemy fire, but neither can we say that the private is more crucial to victory than the general. We can't say that victorious troops marching into a newly liberated town are more heroic than those who were killed before victory had been won, but we also wouldn't want to take anything away from the accomplishment of the soldiers who survived and pressed forward until victory was achieved. It's hard to say what kind of hero is best.

But what if there was a person who somehow managed to do all these things? What if there was a general who devised a brilliant strategy, who courageously placed himself at the point of the fiercest conflict, who was tortured and killed, and yet who could somehow defeat the cruelest enemy, enjoy a victory parade, and bring freedom, justice, peace, and prosperity to millions throughout the entire earth? Wouldn't such a person be the ultimate war hero? No mere human could do all that, of course, but there is one person, both human and divine, who has indeed accomplished all these things. His name is Jesus Christ, and he is the ultimate war hero.

The Lord is a Warrior

The Old Testament tells many stories of how the Lord defeated his enemies and rescued his people. The Lord wiped out the armies of Pharaoh at the Red Sea, and the people of Israel sang, "The Lord is a warrior" (Exodus 15:3). When the Israelites fell into the cruel oppression of the Canaanites, the Lord rescued them and gave them a great victory near a place called Har-Meggido, or Armageddon, inspiring his people to sing, "So may all your enemies perish, O Lord!" (Judges 5:31). The Lord brought down the walls of Jericho; he destroyed the giant Goliath; he wiped out the cruel armies of Assyria, killing 185,000 troops in a single night. And those are just a few of the Lord's warrior deeds in the Old Testament. People of faith knew God as a mighty commander of vast armies. They prayed for him to show his power, defeat his enemies, and rescue his people.

What the Old Testament says about the Lord God, the New Testament applies to the Lord Jesus. In Jesus the being of God is joined to a human individual. Jesus was humble, gentle, and willing to sacrifice himself to save others, but that doesn't mean the Lord stopped being a warrior. Coming to earth was Jesus' way of entering territory occupied by the enemy forces of Satan and setting in motion a strategy for bringing millions of people over to the side of God and setting them free forever. Although he was supreme commander, Jesus suffered more than anyone under his command when he was captured, tortured, and killed. That was not the end of him, however. Dying on the cross was Jesus' way of paying for the sins of those he had come to save, and it was also his way of disarming Satan and dooming him to defeat. Jesus rose from the dead, breaking the grip of sin, death, and Satan, and he now reigns in power, poised for the final offensive when the time is right.

In the last book of the New Testament, Revelation, the apostle John sees a vision of Jesus the war hero. "I saw heaven standing open," writes John, "and there before me was a white horse, whose rider is called Faithful and True. With justice he judges and makes war... the armies of heaven were following him" (Revelation 19:11-14). In the visions of Revelation, General Jesus faces the forces of Satan and all the leaders and armies this wicked world can muster in a final Armageddon. Christ overcomes all his enemies with a blast of divine power and casts them into the fire of hell forever. Then he brings heaven to earth and gives his people eternal peace and joy.

General Jesus is gentle and generous toward his friends, but he's devastating to those who refuse to join his side. Jesus is not only a wise teacher and kind helper; he's also the ultimate war hero, supreme in strategy, bravery, sacrifice, and victory.

Strategy, Bravery, Sacrifice, Victory

As a commander and strategist, the Lord came up with a plan that no merely human general could have conceived, a plan brilliant enough to astonish even the angels. Throughout human history there have been some talented military leaders who have devised some clever strategies, but none except Jesus could devise a strategy to conquer sin, death, and Satan. No general could ever surpass the strategic brilliance of General Jesus.

And that's not all. Jesus is supreme not only in strategy but also in humility and bravery. A general who comes up with a brilliant plan usually leaves it to others to actually carry out the most dirty and dangerous part of the plan. What general would stoop to the dirty work of polishing the boots of those under his command? But that's what Jesus did when he washed the dirty feet of his disciples. What general would expose himself to the greatest danger and send himself behind enemy lines on a mission that is sure to get him killed? But that's what Jesus did. No war hero could ever surpass the humility of Jesus in performing the lowliest task for others of lower rank, and no war hero could ever surpass the bravery of Jesus in handling the deadliest assignment himself.

As the ultimate war hero, Jesus made the ultimate sacrifice. If a group of soldiers was trapped and one of them deliberately showed himself and drew enemy fire and died to give his friends a chance to slip away, it would be heroic. If a live grenade landed among some troops and one of them flung himself on the grenade in order to absorb the blast and save his friends, it would be heroic. But even such sacrifices as these are surpassed by the sacrifice of Jesus. Jesus' beatings, torture, and crucifixion brought him enormous pain, and that wasn't the worst of it. He somehow absorbed an eternity's worth of agony as he took the sin of millions upon himself and suffered hell on the cross. If dying to save someone else is the supreme sacrifice, then the hellish death of Jesus makes him the ultimate war hero.

But there is still another aspect of Jesus' heroism to consider: the magnitude of his victory. Jesus is a hero not just because of his death but because of his resurrection, reign, and final victory over all his enemies.

How is the greatness of a victory measured? One measure would be the cruelty and strength of the enemy. It's a greater victory to defeat a huge, well-trained, well-equipped military force than to overcome a small ragtag band that is poorly armed. The more terrible the enemy, the greater the victory. If we measure the magnitude of Jesus' victory by the power of the enemy he defeats, no other war hero can compare to Jesus.

The book of Revelation pictures Christ's enemies as awful and powerful. The Lord and his people aren't up against harmless, helpless opponents. No, the enemies are brutal and powerful, and there are plenty of them. Revelation portrays at least five different kinds of opposition. One is a hideous dragon, representing Satan himself. Another is a vicious beast which does the dragon's dirty work, an antichrist oppressor who represents the worst cruelty and persecution. Then there's a beastly false prophet, using false religion and phony miracles and joining forces with the powers of persecution. A fourth enemy mentioned in Revelation is a prostitute named Babylon who seduces countless people and drinks the blood of Christians; she represents worldly culture with its corrupting, killing effects. Joining these dreadful powers is a fifth element: multitudes of people and armies who reject Christ and his cause.

If you read Revelation and focus mainly on the enemies of Christ, it can be terrifying. But the main point of showing these enemies in all their power and terror is to show what a great victory Christ wins in defeating such enemies. When all the powers of earth and hell seem to be against you, it's tempting just to give up. How can anybody resist? If you can't beat them, join them, right? But any such thoughts vanish when you see the ultimate war hero, the rider on the white horse, Jesus himself, and see his awesome power to crush all his enemies.

Defeating Dreadful Enemies

The book of Revelation records various visions involving the dragon, the beast, the false prophet, the prostitute Babylon, and the armies of sinners who oppose Christ. These visions all have something in common: they all end with the enemy being defeated and punished and Christ reigning triumphant.

Some Bible scholars try to apply each vision to a different phase of the future, but perhaps the best way to see these visions is to understand them as describing the same conflict from various perspectives. In that sense it would be like watching a film which shows a single battle but which deals first with one part of the battlefield, then shifts to another, then back again, focusing on different actors, using various camera angles, sometimes showing how one part of the battle goes and then flashing back in order to show how another part of the battle was unfolding at the same time.

The dragon, the beast, and the false prophet gather the kings of the earth and their armies, all of them in league with Babylon, and they come together at Armageddon. Revelation then portrays the outcome of the battle. First the fall of Babylon, the prostitute civilization, and her allies is envisioned. Then comes another vision, focusing on the defeat of the beast and the false prophet. Still another vision focuses especially on the defeat of Satan the dragon and the people who sided with him against Christ and his people. These visions show different aspects of the same event: the final victory of Jesus Christ when he comes again to judge the world.

Just before the coming of Jesus, his enemies may seem to have the upper hand. The cause of Christ may appear hopeless. His people may seem surrounded and helpless. But when Christ himself appears in majesty and might, the power of his enemies will suddenly seem as nothing. The earth will shake and Babylon, the city and culture which seemed so great, will collapse in a moment. The beast and the false prophet, the powers of persecution and deception at their worst, will instantly be helpless and hell bound. Revelation 19 says,

> I saw heaven standing open and there before me was a white horse, whose rider is called Faithful and True. With justice he judges and makes war. His eyes are like blazing fire, and on his head are many crowns. He has a name written on him that no one knows but he himself. He is dressed in a robe dipped in blood, and his name is the Word of God. The armies of heaven were following him, riding on white horses and dressed in fine linen, white and clean. Out of his mouth comes a sharp sword with which to

strike down the nations. "He will rule them with an iron scepter." He treads the winepress of the wrath of God Almighty. On his robe and on his thigh he has this name written: KING OF KINGS AND LORD OF LORDS...

Then I saw the beast and the kings of the earth and their armies gathered together to make war against the rider on the white horse and his army. But the beast was captured, and with him the false prophet who had performed the miraculous signs on his behalf. With these signs he had deluded those who had received the mark of the beast and worshiped his image. The two of them were thrown alive into the fiery lake of burning sulfur. The rest of them were killed with the sword that came out of the mouth of the rider on the horse, and all the birds gorged themselves on their flesh.

The magnitude of Jesus' victory is apparent when you see the enormous strength of his enemies and see how quickly Jesus defeats them all when he unleashes his might.

The most terrible enemy is Satan himself, but even Satan doesn't stand a chance against the ultimate war hero. In Revelation 20 the Bible pictures the role that Satan plays in the last battle and what happens to him. Satan deceives people from all over the world and gathers them for battle.

In number they are like the sand on the seashore. They marched across the breadth of the earth and surrounded the camp of God's people, the city he loves. But fire came down from heaven and devoured them. And the devil, who deceived them, was thrown into the lake of burning sulfur, where the beast and the false prophet had been thrown. They will be tormented day and night for ever and ever (Revelation 20:8-10).

If an army combining every deadly demon and hateful human can't stand against the Lord in the last battle, surely any lesser forces will never defeat Christ or prevent his final victory.

This means that if you don't belong to Jesus Christ, you are doomed. Revelation speaks of those who wear "the mark of the beast," and some authors work hard to figure out what such a mark might be. But let's not make it too complicated. All who don't bear the mark of baptism or live by faith in Christ end up wearing the mark of the beast. Their names are not in the book of life. This applies not only to the end of history but to every point before the end. There's a war going on right now; the last battle will simply be the fiercest and final part of the war. Those who are defeated in the last battle will end up in the fires of hell, and those who even now choose the wrong side in the long war leading up to the last battle will also end up in hell.

On the other hand, those who, by God's grace, are on the side of Christ may be sure of victory. The Bible's visions of the last battle speak to God's people in every age. We don't need to know when the final battle will be. We need to take sides with Christ right now and do so with confidence. For if the Lord will someday take on all the fiercest powers of evil all at the same time and defeat them quickly and totally, then he will surely be able to save us from any lesser attacks we might face in the time before the last battle.

Some folks want to use the Bible's visions to figure out how close we might be to the end of history. But nobody can figure this out with any accuracy, and that's not the most important thing. What's important is that, no matter when the end might come, we must be on the side of Christ right now and realize that all the rage of earth and hell cannot overcome the ultimate war hero.

Fruits of Victory

The greatness of a victory is seen in what strong enemies are defeated, and another measure of the greatness of a victory is the amount of good it produces. The allied victory in World War II, for example, was a greater thing for Western Europe than for Eastern Europe. In Eastern Europe, people merely got Stalin instead of Hitler, while in Western Europe people gained freedom, peace, and a return to prosperity. A victory that produces liberty, justice, and even joy is far greater than a victory that merely produced a new brand of oppression.

Here again Jesus shines as the ultimate hero. Revelation says that the victory of Jesus leads to a new heaven and a new earth, with "no more death or mourning or crying or pain" (21:4). The new creation will have as its capital the holy city, New Jerusalem, a place of astonishing beauty and security. God's people will be filled with his light and life and enjoy face-to-face friendship with the Lord for all eternity. They will enjoy prosperity and authority beyond imagination, reigning with Christ forever.

Of all the heroes who have fought to make the world a better place, only the Lord Jesus can succeed completely. Only Christ can make the world a perfect place of uninterrupted harmony, holiness, and happiness. And you will be part of that perfect world if Christ is your Savior and Commander right now.

Meanwhile, the war between good and evil isn't over, but D-Day has already happened. Jesus invaded this world by coming here as a man, absorbing the deadly attacks of Satan, sin, and death, and making the decisive breakthrough in his resurrection. Now the victory of good over evil is sure. It's just a matter of time. Think again of World War II. After D-Day there were still other battles to be fought, some of them quite awful, but the final outcome of the war had been determined on D-Day. So too, after Jesus' death and resurrection, the war between good and evil still continues, and some of the battles are awful. But the outcome has been decided by Jesus' first coming, and the Lord has given us a glimpse of his victorious second coming. So, no matter how fierce the conflict may still be, the final outcome is sure.

The Bible portrays Jesus as the ultimate war hero, unsurpassed in strategy, humility, bravery, sacrifice, and victory. The Bible pictures Jesus this way to give him the honor and praise he deserves, to call Jesus' enemies to surrender and join his side before it's too late, and to encourage Jesus' followers that we are more than conquerors through him who loved us. Do you trust Jesus as *your* ultimate hero?

Chapter Three

Call to Combat

Be strong in the Lord and in the power of his might.
(Ephesians 6:10)

Jesus Christ is a general. The church is a fighting force. Christian people are soldiers. Christian living is war. The call to become a Christian is a call to combat. It's a call to enlist in the forces of General Jesus, to fight his enemies, to pursue his strategy and objectives, to wear his protective gear and attack with his weapons.

If you think Jesus came into the world to make it instantly peaceful and comfortable, think again. Jesus says, "I did not come to bring peace but a sword" (Matthew 10:34). Jesus came to start a fight, and he has already won the decisive battle. But the war isn't over yet. Jesus calls people to join his forces and march with him to final victory. The outcome is certain, but the fighting still rages, and there can be no peace until every stronghold falls and the last enemy is defeated. Only when the war is over can we enjoy the benefits of peace and freedom. Until then we live in a combat zone. We must fight for Jesus, or else we are against him. It is impossible to be neutral.

Does this sound too aggressive and violent? At some points in history, bloody religious wars have been fought under the sign of the cross, and terrible crimes have been committed in the name of Jesus. But that's not the kind of combat Jesus calls for. It is impossible to change hearts by force. When Christ calls people to combat, it is warfare of a very different kind.

We must fight spiritual enemies, and we must use spiritual weapons. The enemy is not a nation or its military; the enemy is far worse. The war is not conflict between nations; the powers involved are greater than any nation. The weapons are not guns and blades and bombs that destroy humans; the Lord's weapons blast the bunkers of evil and devastate demons. "For the weapons of our warfare are not of the flesh but have divine power to destroy strongholds. We destroy arguments and every lofty opinion raised against the knowledge of God, and take every thought captive to obey Christ" (2 Corinthians 10:4-5). Christianity is spiritual warfare, with larger and longer-lasting results than any physical, political war.

Peace in Our Time?

Our warfare is spiritual, not physical—but it is still warfare. We must stand and fight for Christ, not be spiritual appeasers. Spiritual appeasers see no need for conflict, no need for a fight. Some churches are eager to avoid every hint of combat. They don't sing "Onward, Christian Soldiers, Marching as to War" or "Stand Up, Stand Up for Jesus as Soldiers of the Cross" or any other hymn about battling sin and Satan. They don't preach Bible passages that describe Christianity in military language. Why not? Why no mention of spiritual warfare? Some church leaders and their followers don't see Satan as a threat; they might not even believe that Satan and his demons are real. They think human nature is basically good; they see little need to fight sin. They don't see false religion as a danger to souls, they aren't eager to lead non-Christians to a relationship with Jesus, and they oppose vigorous evangelism. Spiritual appeasers think we just have to love ourselves, be tolerant of others, and all will be well.

The Bible says otherwise: I must fight against my own sins and Satan's attacks against me, and I must join Jesus' mission of bringing gospel freedom to others and winning them to his cause. This kind of warfare—fighting Satan in our personal life and spreading gospel freedom to others—does not involve physical force. The Bible allows *government* to use physical force and weapons in some situations, but that is not the *church's* calling. The church must mobilize people not for political and military conflict but for spiritual warfare. When the Bible calls the church and individual Christians to combat, it calls for something very different from the kind of wars and weaponry that make the news. Scripture calls for warfare in the unseen realm: spiritual warfare against Satan and the power of sin. This doesn't require guns, tanks, and fighter jets—but it does require courage, determination, and strength.

There's a lot more to following Jesus than being a nice, tame pussycat. The Bible speaks of Jesus as a lion (Revelation 5:5), and Scripture says, "The righteous are as bold as a lion" (Proverbs 28:1). Do you see Jesus as a lion or as a fluffy kitten? Do you want to be a tame pet in a safe home that does nothing but lie around and eat? Or do you want to be a lion in the service of the ultimate lion, Jesus Christ? To live as a real Christian, it's not enough to be tame and safe. You need to be bold, strong, even fierce.

Lack of this warrior mentality may be one reason many churches have little appeal to men. Instead of God's call to be strong, some churches merely call men to be nice. Author John Eldredge says,

> Christianity, as it currently exists, has done some terrible things to men. When all is said and done, I think most men in the church believe God put them on earth to be a good boy... If they try really hard they can reach the lofty summit of becoming ... a nice guy. That's what we hold up as models of Christian maturity: Really Nice Guys.

Wouldn't Bible study be more exciting if it became a strategy session of warriors? Wouldn't church be different if it became a place to rally for war against Satan? Church might then be a place not just for children, women, and old people, but a place for men—bold, dangerous men who are strong in the Lord and in his mighty power.

In any case, whether the church has turned men off by becoming too wimpy or men have simply hardened their hearts against the Lord, the fact remains that all of us—men and women alike—are living in a spiritual war zone. You might want a peaceful, easy feeling, but if you aren't prepared to fight sin, if you're not ready to battle Satan, if you're not on a mission to win victories for Jesus, you are doomed. You can't negotiate or make peace with Satan.

In the period before World War II, the British government was so eager to avoid conflict that it stood back as Adolph Hitler invaded one country after another. Prime Minister Neville Chamberlain boasted of solving disputes "by discussion instead of by force of arms" and spoke flattering words about Hitler and Mussolini. After the Munich agreement giving Czechoslovakia to Hitler, Chamberlain said, "I believe it is peace for our time. Go home and get a nice, quiet sleep." Many British people cheered wildly. But there would be no peace and little quiet sleep. The only way to stop Hitler was to fight.

When a tyrant wants to conquer everything he can, there can be no peace. Satan is a tyrant, and he wants to conquer everything he can. Satan wants to dominate you and hold you under the power of sin. Satan wants you to die in your sin and end up in hell with him. He wants people around you to perish too. He wants them to ignore Jesus, believe false religions, and end up in hell. If you expect peace in our time, a life without struggle or conflict, Satan will completely control you.

Don't be an appeaser. Be a warrior. Stand against Satan. Fight him. "Be strong in the Lord and in his mighty power. Put on the full armor of God so that you can take your stand against the devil's schemes" (Ephesians 6:10-11). Join Jesus' army, and don't expect an easy, peaceful life. It's hard to stand against Satan's attacks. It's hard to go into enemy-occupied territory and bring the liberty of Christ to those ruled by Satan. There will be no peace in our time. There will be spiritual warfare until Jesus comes again.

His Mighty Power

The first and most important thing about spiritual warfare is to look to the strength and leadership of the ultimate war hero. Scripture says plainly, "The Lord is a warrior" (Exodus 15:3). Why did Jesus come to earth? To pick a fight! Jesus says, "I did not come to bring peace but a sword" (Matthew 10:34). The final result of Jesus' coming will be peace, but before he brings peace, he brings a sword against evil, and he brings division between those who join him and those who reject him.

Jesus did not come to earth to negotiate with Satan. He did not come for diplomacy or to work out a compromise. Jesus came to destroy. "The reason the Son of God appeared was to *destroy* the devil's work" (1 John 3:8). The Son of God became one of us and died for us "to *destroy* him who holds the power of death—that is, the devil" (Hebrews 2:14).

Do you think of the Lord as a warrior, as a destroyer of his enemies? In the Bible, God often reveals himself that way, and biblical prayers speak of him that way. Psalm 18 starts out with words of love—"I love you, O Lord"—but is this love for a sugary, sentimental deity? No, he's the God of strength and battle. The psalmist says, "I love you, O Lord, *my strength*," and then says,

The Lord thundered from heaven; the voice of the Most High resounded. He shot his arrows and scattered the enemies, great bolts of lightning and rout-

ed them... With your help I can advance against a
troop; with my God I can scale a wall... You armed
me with strength for battle (Psalm 18).

Psalm 68 speaks of God's concern for orphans and widows, but does that mean God is just a gentle do-gooder?
No, one reason God is such a comfort to the weak is that
he wields terrifying power against enemies:

May God arise, may his enemies be scattered, may
his foes flee before him... A father to the fatherless,
a defender of widows, is God in his holy dwelling... The chariots of God are tens of thousands
and thousands of thousands... Surely God will
crush the heads of his enemies... Summon your
power, O God; show us your strength, O God as
you have done before (Psalm 68).

The Lord Jesus calls us to join his fight against Satan
and evil, against sin, cruelty, fear, discouragement, and all
Satan's other weapons. Jesus could be very gentle with
weak and wounded souls, but he could also be combative
and downright terrifying to Satan and his demons. Jesus
often met people who were possessed and tormented by
demons. These people did not have the strength to liberate
themselves from demonic power. But Jesus had more than
enough strength, and the demons knew it. They panicked
whenever they saw Jesus coming. Some demons yelled in
rage; some whimpered in fear; all felt threatened by Jesus.
They knew they could not stand against him. As the Bible
says of the Lord, "How awesome are your deeds! So great
is your power that your enemies cringe before you" (Psalm
66:3). Demons are not wimps. They are rebel angels who
have lost all goodness but still have terrible strength. Human power can't scare them, but the divine power of Jesus
terrifies them. In fact, Jesus only had to speak a few words
to make the demons flee.

If you've always thought of Jesus as a mild-mannered
wimp, please watch the real Jesus in action. When he's

confronted by a legion of demons, Jesus sends them flee-
ing in terror (Luke 8:26-33). When he's told that King
Herod wants to kill him, Jesus fearlessly denounces the
wicked king (Luke 13:32). When he's told that his words
have offended some elite religious leaders, Jesus offends
them even more by calling them "blind guides" (Matthew
15:12-14). When he sees God's temple made into a marketplace, Jesus goes on a rampage with a whip, driving out
the merchants and flipping their tables upside down (John
2:15). When he sees a mob coming to arrest him, Jesus
calmly tells them that he's the one they're after—and
something about him makes them shrink back and fall to
the ground (John 18:3-6). When Jesus enters death itself
and takes on the ultimate enemy, the ground shakes, the
grave opens, and death is defeated. These are not the ac-
tions of a passive, harmless wimp. This is the Lord of
hosts, the commander of angels, the ruler of the kings of
the earth, the General who calls us to combat in his forces.

The Bible pictures Jesus as a general riding a white
horse, with the armies of heaven following him. If you've
seen *The Two Towers*, the second film in *The Lord of the
Rings* trilogy, think of the great battle scene where a mon-
strous army is launching a terrible assault on Helm's Deep.
The weary, wounded defenders have little hope for success, but they won't give up, and they try a desperate coun-
terattack. At that very moment, a rider on a white horse
appears at the top of a hill, followed by a mighty army. It is
their friend Gandalf, racing to help. On their own, the defenders could not win, but once the rider on the white
horse shows up, they can't lose. The enemy is crushed.
That's just a hint of how the ultimate rider on the white
horse, Jesus Christ, has power to defeat the forces of Satan.

Be Strong

That same power can be yours and mine—not because
we're divine or equal to Jesus, but because Jesus gives the

power of his Holy Spirit to those who trust him. When Scripture says, "Be strong in the Lord and in his mighty power," it means that we can be strong in the very same power that enabled Jesus to terrify demons and to defeat death. God calls us to be strong, not on our own, but in the strength of Christ. Expect victory, not because you're so strong on your own, but because you're part of the irresistible forces of Jesus. This is warfare for winners.

If you've been bullied by evil power, you may realize that Satan is much stronger than you are, and you might find it hard to believe that Satan will ever be defeated or that you will ever be free. Even after Jesus has entered the conflict, even though Satan is losing ground and is doomed to destruction, you still might have a hard time believing it. The good news of the gospel might not be getting through to you. Satan is losing, but he won't tell you that. He'll do everything he can to keep you from finding out about his defeat at the hands of Christ.

Satan has dominated so many of us for so long that we find it hard to believe in the defeat of evil and in our liberation. We find it hard to believe that our struggle is warfare for winners. Even as his power collapses, Satan keeps telling lies. He whispers into our minds that we are losers. He keeps saying that Jesus is dead. He keeps tempting us to side with evil rather than with Christ. Satan tries to keep us from finding out the real truth about his defeat so that we won't rise up against him and shake off the shackles of sin. But the gospel announces the triumph of Christ, the defeat of Satan, and the call to be free of a dying regime. The gospel calls us to accept the rule of Christ and to rejoice in freedom from sin and fear. Don't be intimidated by lies that the forces of evil are winning. Satan is too strong for you or me, but a far greater power has entered the battle. Satan is no match for Jesus and his angel armies.

The Lord is a warrior, and he calls you to join him in the warfare against the spiritual forces of evil. Be brave and fierce in resisting evil. "Be strong in the Lord and in his mighty power." Join Jesus in demolishing Satan's crumbling regime. Psalm 144:1-2 says, "Praise be to the Lord my Rock, who trains my hands for war, my fingers for battle. He is my loving God and my fortress, my stronghold and my deliverer, my shield, in whom I take refuge, who subdues peoples under me." Psalm 149:6 says, "May the praise of God be in their mouths and a double-edged sword in their hands." The day of peace will come when Christ returns, but in this day of battle, we have the heroic calling to battle against sin, doubt, and despair, and to tell others the good news that Satan is losing and that they can be free from his tyranny and enjoy freedom under the loving leadership of Jesus Christ.

Are you taking your stand or just taking a nap? Have you put on the armor of God, or have you refused to join his forces? This is no time for indecision. It is no time for cowardice. It is no time for appeasement. It is time to accept Jesus as your leader and to become a daring, dangerous soldier in his army. You might think it's ridiculous even to imagine yourself as daring and dangerous. But if you dare to live by faith, you are an extreme danger to Satan and his demons. You have a very strong Father—the Lord is a warrior—and you can be a strong warrior who stands firm in faith. So be bold. Strike fear into Satan. Keep capturing more territory for General Jesus. Be strong in the Lord and in his mighty power.

Chapter Four

Armed and Ready

Therefore put on the full armor of God, so that when the day of evil comes, you may be able to stand your ground, and after you have done everything, to stand.

(Ephesians 6:13)

It was a dark and stormy night—about as stormy as any night could get. Snow and sleet slashed the air. The weather was too bad to be outside. It was Christmas, a night to stay inside and party, so the soldiers stationed in Trenton, New Jersey, decided to relax and have fun. They didn't want to be outside, and they were sure no enemy would venture outside in such weather.

The soldiers in Trenton were Hessians, professional fighting men from Germany. They were in Trenton the winter of 1776 because they had been hired to join British forces and stamp out the rebellion of the pesky American colonists. The Hessians had easily won several clashes with the Americans and scoffed at the ragtag colonists. The Hessian troops in Trenton didn't even bother to build up fortifications or have a safe place for baggage in case of attack. They figured they could easily destroy any Americans who might attack them.

That night in particular, they were sure there would be no attack. George Washington and his men were on the other side of the Delaware River, and that's where they would surely stay. What madman would dream of crossing the river on such a night? It was horrible to be outdoors at all, let alone try to steer boats through dark waters made more dangerous by jagged slabs of floating ice. Even if they made it across the river, they'd have to walk nine miles in the horrible weather to reach Trenton. This was one night the Hessian soldiers didn't have to think about combat. They could afford to kick back and party until the wee hours of the morning.

They didn't know George Washington. While the Hessians were gobbling food and guzzling barrels of beer and rum—just as General Washington figured they would be doing—the general set his plan in motion. He and his men braved the bitter cold, climbed into boats, and made their way across the treacherous Delaware River. Many of the men hardly had enough clothing to stay warm. But Washington kept encouraging them, and at last they were gathered on the other side of the river. Then they made the nine-mile march to Trenton.

By the time they arrived, the night was over, and they feared they had lost the opportunity for a surprise attack. But most of the Hessians were still in bed. Their commander was groggy from heavy drinking the night before. Washington's men subdued the Hessians after a short skirmish and captured more than a thousand prisoners. It was a major victory in the war for American independence.

It was also a lasting lesson that if you're a soldier, you must be armed and ready. It's not enough to have equipment available somewhere. You must be armed with that equipment and be able to use it. A soldier can't prepare only for nice weather and comfortable conditions; he must be ready to fight any time, under any conditions. That was the key to the American victory over the Hessians. That's also the key to victory in spiritual warfare: You must be armed and ready to fight at any time, under any conditions.

Ready for the Evil Day

In Ephesians 6, the Bible calls God's people to "be strong in the Lord and in his mighty power" and to recognize that our worst enemy is not any human person or country but "the spiritual forces of evil" led by Satan. "Therefore," commands Ephesians 6:13, "put on the full armor of God, so that when the day of evil comes, you may be able to stand your ground, and after you have done everything, to stand." You never know when that day of evil will come. You never know when you'll have to fight. So be armed and ready at all times to battle Satan.

Don't be caught napping, Scripture says, "Let us not be like others, who are asleep, but let us be alert and self-controlled" (1 Thessalonians 5:6). The Hessian troops at Trenton had plenty of supplies and training, but all the supplies and training in the world won't help soldiers who are sleeping off a drunken hangover when the enemy attacks. Likewise, we have plenty of God-given supplies, protection, and weapons available to us, but the armor of God doesn't help people who aren't wearing it and are sleeping. Satan can sneak up on you, and battle can break out when you least expect it. The Bible says, "Be prepared in season and out of season" (2 Timothy 4:2). Be prepared every day, even on the least likely day for an attack, so that if it turns out to be the evil day of Satan's assault, you can stand firm.

Sometimes the day of evil comes in the form of a painful illness or disability. If you always assumed you'd stay healthy and happy and never prepared yourself for such things, you'll be caught by surprise and your faith may fall when your health fails. But if you arm yourself in advance by learning what the Bible says about suffering and by trusting God's promises, you can stand firm.

Sometimes the day of evil comes as the tragic death of a loved one. If you always assumed that such things would never affect *you*, the blow may be too much for you to bear. You may turn against God and surrender to Satan's anger and despair. But if, when things are going well, you take the Lord as your comfort in life and in death, and if you keep strengthening your faith by focusing on Jesus' resurrection power, then you'll be ready to defeat Satan when death strikes close to you.

Sometimes the day of evil comes in the form of persecution. If you assume that nobody would mock Christian beliefs or the Christian way of life, if you assume you would never lose a job or face hardship for following Jesus, you may be caught by surprise when persecution hits you. But if you're prepared in advance, knowing that when you join Jesus' army you'll be targeted for attack, then you'll have your armor on and be able to stand up under persecution without abandoning the Lord.

Sometimes the day of evil comes as temptation to sin. You may be tempted to cheat on classwork or to make money by crooked methods or to have sex with someone who isn't your spouse or to gossip about others or you may be tempted by something else, but whatever it is, Satan presents something that seems so delicious, so desirable, so necessary for your happiness, that if you're not fortified in advance to resist temptation, you will fall into sin. But if you're fortified by study of God's law in Scripture and by the strength of God's Holy Spirit inside you, then you can say no to the tempter and defeat his strategy.

Sometimes the day of evil comes as lies about God. Satan attacks with all sorts of false doctrines and deceptive theories, and if you're not protected by knowledge of God's truth, you can fall for Satan's lies. But if you know your Bible and your mind is clothed in the truth of Christ, you can repel Satan's lies.

In all of this, you need to be ready in advance. Don't wait to get ready until after the attack starts; prepare for battle ahead of time. Be ready for suffering *before* it strikes. Be ready for tragedy *before* it strikes. Be ready for persecution *before* it strikes. Be ready for temptation *before* it comes. Be ready for doctrinal challenges *before* they arise. Put on the full armor of God *before* Satan attacks you.

Once the attack has begun, it's rather late to be looking around for armor and weapons. Many casualties of spiritual warfare occur, not because the attack was so fierce, but because the person was not prepared ahead of time. If you ignore the Bible when things are going well, it will be hard to find what you need from the Bible when the evil day comes and Satan attacks you. If you don't draw on Jesus' protective power when life is calm and you can think clearly, how will you know what to do when your mind is spinning and your heart is breaking? Put on the full armor of God, keep up your training and combat readiness, keep listening to God's direction, and you will have what it takes to stand against the devil's schemes.

Summer Soldiers?

In spiritual warfare, we must always be armed and ready. Part of our readiness is realism about the difficulty of the struggle. At the time of the American war for independence, there were some colonists who didn't realize how long and hard the war would be. They talked big about freedom and patriotism in the exciting summer when the Declaration of Independence was signed, but they deserted the cause when more of Great Britain's mighty warships and armies arrived. However, others never expected it to be easy. All along they had expected a hard, long struggle. They stood firm in the worst times when others gave up. "These are the times that try men's souls," wrote Thomas Paine. "The summer soldier and the sunshine patriot will, in this crisis, shrink from the service of their country; but he that stands now, deserves the love and thanks of man and woman." The men who crossed the Delaware River in icy darkness with George Washington were not summer soldiers. Those who endured wounds and the bone-chilling winter in Valley Forge were not sunshine patriots. It was men like these who won the victory. Likewise, in the spiritual realm, those who win in the war with Satan are those who can endure hardship and keep battling to the end.

But some religious people don't seem to believe this. They talk as though it's nobler to be a sunshine soldier and a summer saint than to battle Satan in grim circumstances. They have a "name it and claim it" approach in which you just have to speak a few magic words to claim victory, and you can make Satan flee with hardly a struggle. They have a health-and-wealth gospel in which the best Christians are people who don't suffer because their fabulous faith keeps them healthy and prosperous. Their heroes are not strugglers and martyrs but fast-talking preachers with luxury cars and fabulous houses who promise prosperity to their listeners. In their opinion, going through hardship is not a sign of heroism but of weak faith, because, if you're really close to Jesus, faith prevents illness and financial problems, and faith also keeps you from being severely tempted by sin.

But that's nonsense. The Bible says we're in a war. Wartime living isn't always easy, painless, and trouble-free. You can't just "name and claim" victory or "let go and let God." You must fight. Of course you must depend on God's power, not your own, but you still must fight with all the strength God gives you. Living for Jesus is warfare, not a vacation cruise.

Winston Churchill became prime minister of England in the midst of a terrible war with the powerful Nazi forces of the evil Adolph Hitler. The previous prime minister, Neville Chamberlain, had promised "peace in our time" and told his people to "get a nice, quiet sleep." But when war came, it was no time for false peace and phony comfort. Winston Churchill did not promise pleasant times and easy victory. He told his nation,

I have nothing to offer but blood, toil, tears, and sweat. We have before us an ordeal of the most grievous kind... You ask, what is our aim? I can answer in one word. It is victory. Victory at all costs—victory in spite of all terrors. Victory, however long and hard the road may be.

Suppose Churchill had said, "The Nazis are wimps. We can easily defeat them. It won't take much effort or pain." Anyone who expected a quick, easy victory would have given up when in the face of fierce Nazi attacks. But because Britain's leader told his people ahead of time what to expect—blood, toil, tears, and sweat—the troops and people of England stood firm and reached their goal: victory.

Jesus promises victory in our war with Satan, and this outcome is guaranteed by his winning the decisive battle through his death and resurrection. But in promising victory, Jesus does not promise it will be quick and easy. He does not promise health and wealth to those who name it and claim it. He promises blood, toil, sweat, and tears. Jesus promises hardship and suffering as we move toward victory over Satan. Scripture says, "Dear friends, do not be surprised at the painful trial you are suffering, as though something strange were happening to you. But rejoice that you participate in the sufferings of Christ, so that you may be overjoyed when his glory is revealed" (1 Peter 4:12-13).

Don't be shocked when Satan attacks and life is hard. You're in a war. Expect attack. Prepare for it. Endure it and stand firm. The Bible says, "Endure hardship with us like a good soldier of Christ Jesus. No one serving as a soldier gets involved in civilian affairs—he wants to please his commanding officer" (2 Timothy 2:3-4). If Jesus is your commander, and if victory over Satan is your goal, stay focused on your mission. A good soldier has to be able to endure hardship and keep his mind free from distractions that hinder his mission and hamper his effectiveness. You can't win victories if you're more concerned about civilian affairs of health and wealth than with Christ your commander. You must focus on the campaign against Satan and on your God-given mission in that campaign.

A Strong Army

Spiritual warfare is hard, but victory is certain for those on the Lord's side. Spiritual warfare requires all our attention and strength, but the ultimate victory is God's. It is God's armor that protects us, God's weapons that fight for us, and God's overall victory which provides the setting for our individual victory.

Scripture says, "Put on the armor *of God*"—not just armor that God gives but armor that God himself wears. The Old Testament says of the Lord, "He put on righteousness as his breastplate, and the helmet of salvation on his head" (Isaiah 59:17). The New Testament tells us to put on "the breastplate of righteousness" and "the helmet of salvation." The armor the Lord wears, we must wear. The weapons the Lord uses, we must use. The mighty power of God must be our power. The divine strength that defended the Lord Jesus from Satan's temptations and enabled Jesus to conquer sin and death must be our strength.

Suppose you face an invasion from hostile forces. Your only weapons are a kitchen knife and a shotgun for hunting birds. Your only vehicle is a used car. Meanwhile, your enemy has machine guns, grenades, artillery, and tanks. When the battle comes, you will have no chance if your weapons are so pitiful and your enemy's weapons are so powerful. But now suppose you are offered the weapons of a superpower: Stealth bombers, cruise missiles, the best tanks, body armor, and training to use all this equipment. Then your enemy's terrible weapons aren't so unbeatable.

Smart soldiers accept God's equipment and God's training to use that equipment. Who would rather go to war in used cars than in tanks? Who would rather go on the attack armed with kitchen knives than with cruise missiles? If you don't use God's armor and weapons, if you battle Satan ill-equipped and unprepared, you cannot win. But if you use God's equipment, go through his training, and follow his orders, you can't lose.

The weapons of human effort have no chance against Satan's weaponry. But with the power of God, the armor of God, and the weapons of God, we have a huge advantage over Satan's forces. Connected to Jesus, you become part of the best-equipped spiritual fighting force in the world. You have the full armor of God, God's own personal armor, available to protect you from the enemy. You have God's own all-powerful weapons to go on the offensive and drive the enemy back. It's not enough for such armor and weapons to be available, however. You must put them on and use them.

Victim or Victor?

As you fight, don't be discouraged if the battle is especially fierce or if you suffer a setback here or a wound there. Rejoice that God entrusts you with a mission where the fighting is fiercest. The greater the opposition you face, the greater the victory when you triumph. The worse the temptations you have to resist, the worse blows you deal to Satan's forces when you succeed.

Even when you falter or fail, the failure isn't final. Keep in mind the overall campaign. Satan might wound you or take you prisoner for a time, but stay loyal to the Lord. Don't let Satan brainwash you into thinking he is winning or that God has abandoned you. Be confident that God is still winning the overall war, and count on him to rescue you. He won't leave behind even one soldier who loves him and is faithful to him. If you pray to him and seek his forgiveness and help, the Lord will rescue you, heal you, and put you back into service. Meanwhile, the outcome of the overall war is already sure. A smart soldier doesn't just look at his own personal success or failure; he looks at how his country and cause is doing. The good news for the Christian soldier is that Jesus is winning, and his cause is assured of victory. Satan is doomed. If individual setbacks trouble you, it helps to remember the big picture. The fight of faith is warfare for winners.

Don't fall into the victim mentality. Many wounded people turn to Jesus and go to church looking for relief from pain and healing for their damaged spirits, and that's good. Jesus offers to heal sin-sick souls and injured spirits. But once he heals you, he doesn't leave you in a hospital bed. Jesus sets you on your feet, trains you for battle, equips you with the full armor of God, and sends you on a mission to do great things for him. The church of Jesus is not just a hospital for victims but an army of victors.

Don't get so stuck in the condition and mindset of a hospital patient that you don't do any soldiering. Every military force has medical units for the wounded, but it also has fighting units, and the fighting units had better be larger than the medical units. A military force is in big trouble if the weak and wounded outnumber those on active duty and ready for combat. If everybody remains as sick as ever, you have to wonder if the doctors know what they're doing. If the officers are content to have all sick patients and no active troops, you have to question whether those officers are fit to lead.

The church is God's army, and the majority of the church ought to be strong and ready for combat, not lying around weak and helpless, depending on pastors to help them survive from day to day. There may have been a time when some churches were too quick to shun sinners and shoot their wounded, but many churches today have gone to the opposite extreme, accepting as normal a situation in which most church people remain broken, pitiable, dysfunctional victims of sin year after year after year. Few are strong in the Lord or strike fear into Satan's forces. This is what happens when the church's motto is merely "find a hurt and heal it" instead of "find a stronghold of Satan and conquer it."

The church must not shoot its wounded members, of course. It must minister to the hurting. Sinners must be restored gently, and doubters must be encouraged. But they must not remain in the same miserable condition. They must become healthy, strong, and ready to take up spiritual weapons in the Lord's mission. If a church prides itself on being compassionate and accepting but doesn't call for transformed lives or lead people to march in Christ's army, it can end up full of people who are mostly sin and little holiness, mostly doubt and little faith. The church becomes like an army where almost everybody is in the hospital and almost nobody is advancing against the enemy. A church that's all therapy, no military, must recover its identity as Christ's army. A person who's always in a pity party and never in a war party, always a weakling and never a warrior, must shake off the victim mentality, draw on Jesus' strength, put on the full armor of God, and learn to stand firm.

The night George Washington and his troops crossed the icy Delaware River and marched on Trenton, many of the men left bloody tracks in the snow from their sore feet and other injuries. They could have sat around feeling sorry for themselves, but instead they attacked the enemy. They were a war party, not a pity party. They focused more on their mission than on their injuries. They focused more on their general's orders than on the harshness of the weather. They focused on the importance of their cause rather than on the power of their enemy. If those patriots had settled into a victim mentality, the war would have been lost. But they were prepared to fight under all conditions, they put their weapons to use, and they won an amazing victory.

Jesus doesn't promise trouble-free victory, but he does promise victory. When you truly commit yourself to his service, you'll be amazed at what you can do in his power. You might say to yourself, "I didn't think I had it in me!"—and you don't have it in you until you get the Holy Spirit of Christ in you. Once the power of Almighty God is in you and his armor surrounds you and his weapons are in your hand, there's no telling what heroic things you can do in his service. You won't do mighty deeds if you're a sunshine soldier or a self-pitying victim. But if you accept Jesus, his armor, and his training, you will be armed and ready for the evil day, and you will be one of the heroes of faith who share in the suffering and the glory of Christ.

Part Two

Evil Enemies:
Devil, World, and Flesh

Your enemy the devil prowls around like a roaring lion looking for someone to devour. Resist him, standing firm in the faith.
(1 Peter 5:8-9)

Everyone born of God overcomes the world. This is the victory that has overcome the world, even our faith. *(1 John 5:4)*

The flesh lusts against the Spirit, and the Spirit against the flesh; and these are contrary to one another. (Galatians 5:17)

From all the deceits of the world, the flesh, and the devil, Good Lord, deliver us.
(Book of Common Prayer)

Chapter Five

The Devil's Attacks

For our struggle is not against flesh and blood, but against the spiritual forces of evil. (Ephesians 6:12)

A pool shark can make hundreds, even thousands, of dollars in a single night, winning bets at barroom billiard tables. What does it take to succeed as a pool shark? At least two things. First, he must be very good at shooting pool. He won't win bets if he can't win games. But he also needs a second skill. He must be a convincing actor and give the impression that he's not that good at pool. If everybody knows how good he really is, nobody will bet against him.

When a pool shark goes into a bar, he tries to blend in. He gives the impression that he's just a regular guy out for a good time. He doesn't usually suggest a bet himself. He lets others suggest the bet and acts reluctant about putting money on the game. Eventually he agrees, and then proceeds to lose (on purpose, of course). Once somebody has beaten him and taken some of his money, they're sure they can beat him again. But when they play again, the shark wins, though not by very much. His opponent is eager for another game of "double or nothing," sure that in the next game he'll win back what he lost. In the end, all the person's money is in the pool shark's pocket.

In all of this, the shark never lets the other person know that he, the shark, is by far the better player. If the shark does it right, he can even come back to the same bar night after night to rake in the money from other victims—or even from the same ones. The shark never shows off how good he really is. He makes sure to miss plenty of shots, though seldom when a game is on the line. He makes sure to lose a game here and there, though never with too much money on the table. He doesn't appear to be much better than those he plays against; the ball just happens to go in for him whenever it matters most. He seems lucky.

But luck has nothing to do with it. The shark has total control of every shot and every game. Even so, his victims, no matter how much they lose, are as sure as ever that he just got lucky and that they can beat him if they play again. They don't realize they never had a chance.

Taking Satan Seriously

Pool sharks remind me of the way Satan operates. Satan is far too much for any mere human to defeat. He is so skilled and strong that his victims don't have a chance, yet so smart and sneaky that his victims seldom know what they're up against. Some people don't believe Satan is real. They don't think the devil and demons even exist. They say it's unrealistic to believe such things. But who is being unrealistic? How can you read history or watch the news and *not* believe Satan and his demons are real? What else explains the dreadful power of evil?

We see smart, sophisticated people get tangled in scandals or trapped by addictions, and we wonder how they could be so stupid; we don't recognize the tempter's cunning. We see wars, terrorism, torture, crime and cruelty, and we wonder how people can be so awful to each other; we don't recognize the devil, whom Jesus described as "a murderer from the beginning" (John 8:44). It's not just a people problem; it's a demon problem. Humans can be sinful and silly, of course, but behind it all lurks demonic evil and deception. The real enemy is Satan.

But we still find it hard to take Satan seriously. We think it's more realistic to believe in our own ability and in that glorious thing called progress. We think we can conquer our problems if only we try just a little harder. We see war and hatred, and we think, "With just a little more negotiation, with just a little more international cooperation, we can make a new world order of peace and security." We see countless children without fathers, we see AIDS destroying millions around the world, and we think, "If we just spend billions of dollars on sex education, things will get better." But the harder we try, the worse it gets.

Who is being realistic: those who think we have human-sized problems with human-sized solutions, or those who believe we're up against something more than human weakness and wickedness, that we face a mysterious enemy of horrifying power? It's amazing that a pool shark can beat someone game after game and take all his money without the victim ever knowing what he's really up against. It's even more amazing that after Satan has done so much damage, many people still don't even think that the devil and his demons are real.

If you can't see Satan's power in crime, conflict, war, and massacres, just look at your own life. Here, too, Satan can be controlling you without you knowing it. He can be taking you for everything you've got, and you still think you can win. You give in to a temptation, and you think, "Oops! That was a mistake, but it won't happen again. Next time I'll do better." You might have a deadly habit. You might have a nasty temper. You might be addicted to pornography. You might abuse your wife or hold grudges or drink too much or have some other rotten habit and think, "This is getting to be a problem, but I can handle it. I just need to try harder. I'll do better next time." All the while, you keep losing to Satan, and he's so sneaky that you don't even know what you're up against.

Like a pool shark, Satan may even let you win once in a while. You resist a temptation, you're okay for a few weeks, and you think, "See, I can do it. I can beat this thing." You don't realize that Satan can beat you any time he wants.

Satan is a former archangel. He has powers you can hardly imagine. He's far more clever and powerful than you or I. He's been in the temptation business for centuries; he's been ruining people for thousands of years, many of them smarter and with greater will power than you or me. And yet you think you can make progress if you just keep trying, if you just give it a little more effort? It would be comical if it weren't so tragic. You'd have better luck against a pool shark.

Satan is real. His demons are real. That's not superstition. It's realism. Read your history. Watch the evening news. Look at your own life. The real enemy isn't just human but demonic. The Bible is utterly realistic when it says, "For our struggle is not against flesh and blood, but against the rulers, against the authorities, against the powers of this dark world and against the spiritual forces of evil" (Ephesians 6:12).

That may sound terrifying—it is terrifying—but it's a major step toward victory to know your opponent, to see your enemy for who he really is. If you have problems with other people, don't focus all your fury on them. See Satan as the real enemy. Also, don't think you can solve your problems on your own, and don't think human progress can solve all our troubles. Satan is too strong to be defeated that way. Depend on God's power to overcome the enemy.

Targeting Demons, Not Humans

Our real enemies are not humans but demons. When you accept this fact, you see people differently. When someone does terrible things and harms you, you might be tempted to hate that person and want him in hell. When you see a certain group of people as the source of everything that's wrong with the world, you might want them to be wiped out. But the real enemy is Satan. He is pushing people to do his dirty work. The main struggle is not against flesh and blood but against spiritual powers.

Picture this: A boy throws a stone at a dog. When the stone strikes, the dog yelps in pain. Then the dog bites the stone furiously to get revenge. But as it bites the stone, the dog ignores the boy who threw the stone. The dog doesn't know the real cause of its pain. That, says John Calvin, is what it's like to ignore Satan and to attack humans who have wronged us. True, they may have hurt us, but Satan is the main culprit, and we should see him as our chief enemy.

If you're fighting a war against a brutal dictatorship, what is a better strategy: to blast civilians who have been dominated by a cruel regime or to go after leaders and military targets? It would be morally wrong and strategically stupid to attack people who are ruled by a horrid regime and not attack the regime itself. A successful strategy would target leadership. The main focus would be fighting strategic command-and-control elements and the hardcore divisions of the enemy military.

If that's the case in ordinary warfare, it's even more important in spiritual warfare. Focus on enemy leadership and on the most hardened, fanatical warriors. The real enemy is Satan and his demons, not people who are caught in the grip of the evil one. Many of those people can still be won over to the Lord's side. Even if humans are on the side of Satan, there is still hope for them. They might live under the power of evil and even serve the cause of evil, but they might become very different if only they are liberated from Satan's tyranny. Satan and his demons are wicked beyond repentance, hardened beyond all possibility of salvation. But most human sinners have not yet reached that point. They might still be saved. God has saved some terrible people in the past and transformed his enemies into his friends, and he can do so again. So whenever you meet a human enemy, you may have to oppose that person, but don't demonize that person. Make the demons your main target, and regard human enemies as potential friends.

This does not excuse human sin. If you sin and go along with Satan, you are responsible. It's no excuse to say, "The devil made me do it," any more than it's an excuse for a soldier who commits war crimes to say, "I was just following orders." If you serve an evil commander and follow his commands, he is responsible, but so are you. If you keep resisting God and siding with Satan, you will meet the same terrible defeat as the demons.

But another possibility is open to you. God gives you an opportunity that he does not give to Satan or his demons. Surrender to Jesus, join the Lord's side, and he will show you mercy and rebuild your life. It is too late for the demons. God's full fury is targeted at Satan's regime, and all demons are doomed to everlasting hell. But it is not too late for you. You have the opportunity to receive God's mercy, abandon the doomed kingdom of evil, and become part of God's kingdom of joy.

God's main battle is not against flesh and blood, so if you're presently God's enemy, you can still become his friend by faith in Jesus. And if you're already God's friend, you should be ready to show other humans the same mercy God has shown you. Jesus tells his followers, "Love your enemies, do good to those who hate you" (Luke 6:27). Knowing that the real enemy is demonic helps us to be more merciful to human enemies.

Effective Weapons

Knowing the real enemy also helps us to depend less on human power and methods and to depend more on God. You and I are up against evil forces of overwhelming power. If all we have is our own best effort, we can't possibly come out on top. You may think it's gloomy and depressing to talk this way. But it's just the opposite! It's glorious to know what the Bible says about Satan. That way he won't be able to fool us any longer, and he won't be able to beat us either, if we use the right weapons.

If the enemy were not so dreadful, the gospel would not be so grand. The glory of the gospel is that God shows us the enemy in all his dreadfulness, and then he announces his victory over Satan and tells how we can share in that victory. The death and resurrection of Christ have dealt Satan a crushing blow. Satan is doomed. With that good news, the Lord calls us to put our faith in Christ, to join the battle against Satan till the victory is complete, and to use the weapons and armor that God provides. We're in a great spiritual battle, and it can only be won with great spiritual weapons. Nothing less will do.

This may sound foolish and backward to some people. They want to be more practical, more relevant. If the problem is war, we need stronger international organizations and better peacekeeping forces. If the problem is crime, we need more police, more prevention, and more sports programs in crime-infested neighborhoods. If the problem is teen pregnancy or sexually transmitted diseases, we need more education. If the problem is an addiction, we need a therapist or support group. If the problem is strange teaching in the church, we need a committee to study the matter. If the problem is bickering, we need a course in interpersonal skills and conflict management.

These things may be good, in some cases they can be helpful, but they're not enough. If we think a flurry of activity and techniques will solve our deepest problems, we're fooling ourselves—or rather, Satan is fooling us. We're in a spiritual war. We face a powerful spiritual enemy. The only way to win is with powerful spiritual weapons. It's tragic when even the church itself forgets this. The

church is tempted to think it can save individuals by becoming just another therapy group or save society by becoming just another political lobby. But Satan laughs if
that's all we fight him with. We're fighting a war with
squirt guns and paper airplanes. We're putting Band-Aids
on gaping wounds.

What the world needs more than anything else, what
you and I need more than anything else, is a gospel that
strikes right at the heart of Satan's evil empire. We need a
gospel that takes Satan seriously, and we need a gospel that
exalts Jesus Christ as the only one who can defeat Satan.
When Jesus called the apostle Paul to preach the gospel to
the world, he said, "I am sending you to them to open their
eyes and turn them from darkness to light, and from the
power of Satan to God, so that they may receive forgiveness of sins and a place among those who are sanctified by faith in me" (Acts 26:17-18). I can't think of a
grander, more urgent, more practical message, than that.
Satan is a dreadful enemy, but he is also a defeated enemy.
There is one thing Satan fears, and that scares him to
death: the gospel of Jesus Christ.

Satan's Schemes
Satan will do anything to keep you from laying hold of
the gospel, because once you do, you will see him for who
he is, you will be aware of his schemes, and you will have
power to defeat him. If you don't believe that Satan is real
and don't depend on Jesus to overcome him, that's just the
way Satan likes it. He will do everything he can to keep it
that way. People sometimes say the reason they don't believe the gospel is that they're free thinkers, well educated,
and progressive. They can't accept the backward, old-
fashioned teachings of the Bible. But unbelief isn't a sign
of intelligence. It's a sign of blindness. Satan "has blinded
the minds of unbelievers, so that they cannot see the light

of the gospel of the glory of Christ, who is the image of God" (2 Corinthians 4:4).

Satan is scared of the gospel. He does all he can to blind you to it, and he does all he can to keep the church from spreading it. He's constantly trying to get church leaders and congregations to leave the biblical gospel behind. Sometimes it works. According to the Bible, "The Spirit clearly says that in later times some will abandon the faith and follow deceiving spirits and things taught by demons" (1 Timothy 4:1). There are those in the church who say that the Bible contains errors. They say Jesus isn't the only way of salvation. They say that there is no Satan and no hell. These people think that they follow the latest scholarship and bring religion up to date. But the truth is that they "abandon the faith and follow deceiving spirits and things taught by demons." Isn't it ironic? They don't believe demons exist, and they're doing the work of demons.

Satan wants to blind you to the truth. He wants the church to forsake the gospel and follow his lies. But what if you believe the gospel anyway, and your church refuses to compromise the truth? What then? Does Satan just give up and take his attacks elsewhere? Dream on! It's often the strongest churches and the most vibrant Christians who are the target of Satan's fiercest attacks.

Satan can't destroy a church built on the gospel, but he can try to disrupt it and make it ineffective, especially if we're not alert to his schemes. He tries to cause arguments and bitterness and division in the church. He arouses suspicion and distrust and dissent. These aren't just human disagreements or personality conflicts. They are the work of Satan. He wants to rob us of our joy and make us miserable. He wants to disrupt our fellowship and destroy our united witness to the glorious gospel of our Lord and Savior. He does all this because he hates the church and because he fears the gospel. He wants to make every biblical church so cranky that it's unpleasant for those inside the church and unattractive to those outside the church.

Let me say it again: Satan's most terrible attacks are often on the strongest churches and the most vibrant Christians. Why? Because he hates them the most and because they are the greatest threat to his power. If you're a Christian, especially if you're eager and active, expect Satan to attack you. Expect that he will even try to make you doubt that you belong to God at all. Some of the godliest Christians, even on their deathbeds, have said that Satan was attacking them with doubts about their salvation. They didn't give in, but that vicious old serpent was taking one last opportunity to hurt them as much as he could.

If you belong to Christ, Satan cannot possibly separate you from God's love or take eternal life away from you, but Satan will do all he can to weaken your joy and your confidence. He does this out of hatred and because he wants you to be so crushed and exhausted that you won't be effective in relation to other people. Satan doesn't want your faith to be joyful, confident, and contagious. He doesn't want other people to hear about Christ from you or to see Christ at work in you. Otherwise, they might believe the great news that they can be saved in Christ and have victory over the devil. That's the last thing Satan wants, so he does all he can to weaken the witness of those who love Christ.

But no matter what Satan tries, don't give in. Don't let him fool you or defeat you. Don't be careless and ignore his power, but don't go to the opposite extreme and despair of ever defeating him. Satan is hateful, he is cunning, he is powerful, but he is also defeated. Jesus is Lord! Satan is scared of Jesus; he is scared of the Holy Spirit; he is scared of the gospel. So "be strong in the Lord and in his mighty power. Put on the full armor of God so that you can take your stand against the devil's schemes." With truth and righteousness and peace and faith and salvation as our armor, with God's Word as our sword, and with the power of prayer to energize us, we can do more to drive Satan back and change this world than all our other efforts combined.

If you've been living without Jesus, if you've been in Satan's grip, maybe without even knowing it, now is the time to change. Now is the time to recognize your real enemy and know what he's been doing to you. Get rid of Satan's domination. Pray for God's salvation. Trust in the Lord Jesus Christ. Welcome his Spirit into your heart. "Submit yourselves, then, to God. Resist the devil, and he will flee from you. Come near to God, and he will come near to you" (James 4:7-8).

Chapter Six

The Devil's Defeat

The reason the Son of God appeared was to destroy the devil's work. (1 John 3:8)

Satan seems to be very active these days. Pastors and counselors encounter people with memories of Satanic ritual abuse. These people recall that when they were children, some adults forced them to be involved in rituals involving blood and black magic and Satan worship. They may even remember being offered to Satan as his property. In many cases it's hard to prove if these things actually happened or if the memories are false. No doubt some people were victims of occult abuse, while others may be victims of horrid illusions planted in their minds by evil powers. Either way, these people feel torn, confused, and in bondage to the powers of darkness.

Other people run up against Satan in a different way. They experiment with the occult and toy with horoscopes, tarot cards, Ouija boards, and séances. They may do it out of curiosity or to get a thrill, and in some cases, it's more of a game to them than anything serious. But some get more than they bargained for. They sink deeper and deeper into the grip of dark powers that are beyond them, and they can't shake themselves free. In the Bible God strongly warns against fortune telling, sorcery, omens, witchcraft, spells, mediums, psychics, and séances to contact the dead (Deuteronomy 18:10-11), but many people ignore the Lord's warnings. People have told me how they got into these things almost as a game at first, but they ended up feeling trapped and terrorized by evil forces.

A disturbing number of young people commit suicide after mixing occult practices with drugs and alcohol and music that focuses on demons and death. Also, some of the most vicious serial killers have been fascinated with the demonic. This can even happen on a political and national scale. There's considerable evidence that Hitler, Hess, Goebbels, and Himmler were deeply involved in occult practices, and so were many other people in Nazi Germany at that time. A number of murderous tyrants were communists who acted in the name of Karl Marx. They claimed not to believe in God or Satan, but they did a lot of Satan's work. There are strong hints that Marx himself sensed the touch of demons. When Marx rejected God, he wrote,

> The hellish vapours rise and fill the brain
> Till I go mad and my heart is utterly changed
> See this sword? The prince of darkness
> Sold it to me.

In another poem Marx wrote,

> Thus heaven I've forfeited
> I know it full well
> My soul once true to God
> Is chosen for hell.

After Friedrich Engels first met Marx, he described him as "a monster possessed by thousands of devils." Was all this talk of being moved by demonic powers just a poetic figure of speech, or was it a hellish reality?

Satan's Many Methods

Satan doesn't just work through occult practices and witches and demon worship. Some of his deadliest schemes are carried out by people who don't believe the devil even exists, who don't resort to black magic or voodoo or rituals involving blood and bats' wings. C.S. Lewis put it this way: "I like bats much better than bureaucrats... The greatest evil is not now done in those sordid 'dens of iniquity'... It is not done even in concentration camps and labour camps. In those we see its final result. But it is conceived and ordered (moved, seconded, carried, and minuted) in clean, carpeted, warmed, and lighted offices, by quiet men with white collars and cut fingernails and smooth-shaven cheeks who do not need to raise their voice."

Perhaps the only thing more dangerous than Satan worshippers are those who don't believe Satan exists. They are educated, sophisticated, efficient—and unaware of who is really calling the shots for them; unaware of the damage they are doing in the service of Satan. To sacrifice a child as part of a demonic ritual in some dark room is no more pleasing to Satan than to abort a child in a well-lit clinic full of stainless steel. To place someone under a voodoo curse is no more pleasing to Satan than to use the finest textbooks and computers to educate a child to think and act as though God doesn't matter.

Satan is equally pleased by those who are obsessed with his power and those who deny his power. In some parts of the world, people live in such fear of demons and witchcraft and magical powers that they will do anything to please those dark forces. In other areas, Satan doesn't have such an easy time scaring people into his service, so he uses the opposite strategy. He keeps a low profile and convinces people that there is no Satan—and maybe no God, either.

That works for a while, but many people find it hard to go on without any religion at all. They feel an urge for something spiritual and supernatural. Satan is waiting to fill the void. He offers an array of non-Christian religions and pagan gods and goddesses and occult practices. He offers New Age ideas that aren't really much newer than Satan himself. When people in nations that were once largely Christian forsake Christ and the Bible, they may at first swing to the extreme of not believing in a spiritual realm at all. But soon many swing to the other extreme and believe in paganism or pantheism.

Satan is very powerful and very tricky. Sometimes he uses witchdoctors, and sometimes he uses corporate executives to do his work. Sometimes he controls people by sheer intimidation, and other times he tells sweet little lies and lures people into temptations and habits they can't seem to break. Sometimes he attacks the church through vicious persecution, and other times he sneaks into the church through false teaching and tries to destroy it from the inside. Satan has many methods but always one goal: to cut people off from God and destroy them.

Satan's Conqueror

I'm not saying all this because I want to focus on Satan. I want to focus on Satan's conqueror, the Lord Jesus Christ. "The reason the Son of God appeared was to destroy the devil's work" (1 John 3:8). The devil is real. We need to know his schemes and realize that he's dangerous. But we also need to know that he's defeated.

How does Jesus defeat the devil and destroy his work? Shortly before Jesus was arrested and crucified, he said, "Now is the time for judgment on this world; now the prince of this world will be driven out. But I, when I am lifted up, will draw all men to myself" (John 12:31-32). By being lifted up on the cross, Jesus would drive Satan back, break the devil's hold on us, and draw people of every kind away from Satan and into relationship with Christ.

When Jesus died on the cross, he defeated Satan and broke the chains of sin and death that held humanity prisoner. All through the time of Jesus' public ministry, he battled with Satan and cast out demons, but those encounters were just skirmishes compared to the decisive battle that was fought at Calvary. On the cross, Jesus drove Satan back and won the victory that decided the outcome of the war once and for all.

It didn't look that way, however. To all appearances, the cross was Satan's greatest victory, the triumph of evil over good. And in a way that's true. It was the devil's hour. But Christ took Satan's finest hour, his greatest victory, and turned it into a devastating defeat. What happened that made Jesus' death such a victory for Jesus and such a defeat for Satan? The Bible describes a number of blows that Jesus dealt to Satan at the cross.

The Tempter Disregarded

First, Jesus disregarded Satan the tempter. The Bible says that Christ was "tempted in every way, just as we are—yet was without sin" (Hebrews 4:15). Early in Jesus' ministry Satan tempted him to take a shortcut to glory. He promised Jesus all the kingdoms of the world, if only Jesus would worship him. No suffering, no humiliation, no need to follow the hard path laid out by God—just instant power. But Jesus refused. Later, Satan spoke again, this time through Jesus' friend Peter, again urging the Lord to follow the path of power rather than humility and suffering. But Jesus said, "Get behind me, Satan."

Finally, the tempter pulled out all the stops as Jesus neared the end. The horror of death and hell loomed in front of Jesus. Would he finally cave in and disobey his Father's plan and take the easy way? Jesus said, "Now my heart is troubled, and what shall I say? 'Father, save me from this hour'? No, it was for this very reason I came to this hour. Father, glorify your name" (John 12:27-28). In the Garden of Gethsemane, Satan's temptation to take the easy way instead of God's way hit Jesus with even greater force, but Jesus prayed, "Father, not my will, but yours be done."

Another of Satan's temptations is to hate and seek revenge on those who hurt us. But again, Jesus disregarded the tempter. Jesus' tormentors slapped him, but he didn't fight back. They mocked him, but he remained silent. The soldiers nailed his hands and feet, but did Jesus give in to hatred? No, he prayed, "Father, forgive them, for they do not know what they are doing" (Luke 23:34). When the onlookers mocked him and told him to come down from the cross, Jesus could have come down then and there and called on thousands of angels to destroy his tormentors. But Jesus knew he had to obey his Father and fulfill the Scriptures, not seek revenge. There at the cross Jesus faced Satan's toughest temptations and disregarded the tempter.

The Liar Disproved

A second blow Jesus dealt Satan at the cross was that he disproved Satan the Liar. Satan would like us to think that the way of this fallen world is really better than God's way, even though it's rooted in sin and disobedience. But at the cross Jesus exposed the world system for what it is: utterly evil and deadly. How did he do that? He stood before the chief priests (representing the world's most advanced religious system) and the Roman governor (representing the world's most advanced legal system), and he brought out the worst in them.

Satan has always wanted the systems and peoples of this world to approve of business as usual, to think they're in touch with true wisdom. At the cross, however, Jesus exposed the fact that they are completely out of touch with true spiritual wisdom. "None of the rulers of this age understood it, for if they had, they would not have crucified the Lord of glory" (1 Corinthians 2:8).

Sometimes we maintain a mask of politeness. Things look okay on the surface, and we'd like to think there's nothing wrong with the way things are. We may even think we're in tune with God. But when God actually showed up in the form of a man, we attacked and killed him. Jesus forced the pretenses to fall away, and at the cross the

world, its people, its religious system, its legal system, and
the devil who calls the shots were all exposed as enemies
of God.

That means big trouble for Satan. He specializes in deception. He doesn't want us to admit our sin or think that
there's anything seriously wrong with a world under his
domination. He'd like us to believe the lie: "I'm okay,
you're okay. Don't worry about what God says." But at the
cross Jesus disproved that lie once and for all. If the world
is okay, it wouldn't have killed Jesus. If I'm okay, and
you're okay, then why did Jesus have to die? At the cross
Jesus disproved the great Liar and exposed sin for what it
is.

The Accuser Dismissed

A third blow Jesus dealt to Satan at the cross is this: he
dismissed Satan the accuser. Satan specializes in extremes.
He tries to get you to believe the lie that sin is no problem
and evil is okay, but if that strategy doesn't work, he tries
to drive you to the other extreme. Satan tries to make you
think your sins are so horrible and you're so rotten and
worthless that there's no hope for you. But at the cross Jesus wrecked that strategy of Satan.

Satan the accuser likes to turn God's law against us and
torment us with our guilt and frighten us with the punish-
ments required by the law. But Jesus took the curse of the
law upon himself. The Bible says, "He forgave us all our
sins, having canceled the written code, with its regulations
that was against us and that stood opposed to us; he took it
away, nailing it to the cross" (Colossians 2:13-14). Jesus
suffered the punishment we deserve. His blood wiped the
record clean. Now when Satan tries to accuse me or drive
me to despair, Jesus defends me. All Satan's charges, all
the evidence he can bring up about how rotten I am—it's
all thrown out of God's courtroom.

Satan leads us into sin. He keeps track of every sin that marks each of us as his property. But when Satan tries to bring charges against us before God, Jesus' blood wipes the whole record clean. That's what happened to the criminal on the cross next to Jesus. Satan had lured that man into a lifetime of crime and wickedness. This man could say nothing in his own defense, and Satan could accuse him of everything in the book. And yet, in the end, this man looked to Jesus, and suddenly there were no more accusations, no more condemnation, just paradise and eternity with God. What a defeat of Satan's strategy! A life-long criminal, home free! The blood of Jesus neutralizes all Satan's work and all his accusations. Every time another person looks to Jesus on the cross and finds that a lifetime of sin is cancelled, the accuser from hell must howl with frustration.

And heaven rejoices. According to the Bible, a loud voice from heaven shouts: "Now have come the salvation and the power and the kingdom of our God, and the authority of his Christ. For the accuser of our brothers, who accuses them before our God day and night, has been hurled down. They overcame him by the blood of the lamb and by the word of their testimony" (Revelation 12:10-11). The blood of Jesus shed on the cross—that's what takes away our guilt and defends us against Satan the accuser.

The Killer Disarmed

Let's look at a fourth blow the devil suffered at Calvary: Jesus disarmed Satan the killer. Satan is like a terrorist, holding us hostage to our fear of death. Death is his most fearsome weapon. But at the cross Jesus disarmed the killer. Jesus entered into death "so that by his death he might destroy him who holds the power of death—that is, the devil—and free those who all their lives were held in slavery to their fear of death" (Hebrews 2:14-15).

The disarming of death became evident the moment Jesus died. "The tombs broke open and the bodies of many holy people who had died were raised to life" (Matthew 27:52). Poor Satan! One moment he was holding death as the ultimate weapon, and the next moment Jesus had disarmed him. Graves were popping open! And now, every time a person dies in Christ, he or she wakes up not in Satan's clutches but in glory, with a splendid resurrection body guaranteed. Satan can't intimidate us through persecution or fear of death any more. We can live our lives in the certainty that neither demons nor death nor anything else in all creation can separate us from the love of God in Christ Jesus our Lord (Romans 8:37-39).

The Mocker Disgraced

Still another aspect of Jesus' victory over Satan is that Jesus disgraced Satan the mocker. Satan's original sin is pride, but at the cross Jesus made the proud prince of this world look utterly ridiculous. The Bible says, "And having disarmed the powers and authorities, [Jesus] made a public spectacle of them, triumphing over them by the cross" (Colossians 2:15).

Satan always mocks a "goody-goody." He makes evil seem so daring and exciting. But Jesus turned the tables, and Satan was the one who ended up being disgraced. At first almost everyone was mocking Jesus as he hung on the cross. But then what happened? After Jesus died, a sense of shame descended on the people when they began to realize what they had done. "When all the people who had gathered to witness this sight saw what took place, they beat their breasts and went away" (Luke 23:48). Right there, in Satan's proudest moment, his servants were filled with shame and disgrace.

That was just a glimpse of the shame Satan was enduring in the spiritual realm. The devil had given it his best shot and failed. Jesus disregarded the tempter, he disproved the liar, he defended against the accuser, he disarmed the killer, and in the process he disgraced the proud mocker.

The Tyrant Dethroned

A final blow Jesus inflicted on Satan at the cross was that Jesus dethroned Satan the tyrant. Satan's power is broken. Now his defeat is sure. The war isn't quite over, but the decisive battle has been won. Satan's power is crumbling. The Bible shows that when Jesus died, Satan's victims were liberated one after another. The thief on the cross beside Jesus went from sin to paradise. The mockers went away ashamed of themselves. The officer who supervised the execution suddenly exclaimed, "Surely, this man was the Son of God" (Mark 15:39). Then two rich politicians who were interested in Jesus but afraid to identify with him—Nicodemus and Joseph of Arimathea—refused to hold back any longer. As they saw Jesus' body hanging there, they stepped forward to be counted among Jesus' friends, and they placed Jesus' body in a tomb. They decided they would rather die with Jesus than live with Satan's way of operating. And what happened out in the cemetery? Graves were popping open!

From there it only got worse for Satan. A few days later, Jesus rose from the dead. He ascended to the throne of heaven and poured out his Holy Spirit on his followers. He sent them out to tell others of his victory, "to open their eyes and turn them from darkness to light, and from the power of Satan to God" (Acts 26:18). The news has kept spreading ever since. The devil is defeated. Satan can't win.

But, you might wonder, if that's true, why are there still so many troubles and horrors in the world, such as those I mentioned earlier? It sure seems the devil is alive and well. But the Bible explains: Satan "is filled with fury, because he knows that his time is short" (Revelation

12:12). He's doomed, so he's doing all the damage he can in the time he has left.

Satan is still powerful and dangerous, but he *is* defeated. He's living on borrowed time. There's no way he can survive what Christ did to him at the cross. Satan is already restricted in what he can do, and in the end, God will cast him into the lake of fire.

In the meantime, don't let Satan bluff you. He's not winning. He's already lost. He's not the greatest power in the universe. Jesus is. Maybe you've been in the grip of occult or voodoo or demonic powers, but those powers can't hold you when you look to Christ and his cross. Maybe you're in the grip of habits that seem unbreakable, but don't despair. Jesus has broken Satan's power, and he can set you free. Maybe you think the outlook for the world is hopeless, but think again. Trust Jesus. He has already won the victory by his death and resurrection.

Chapter Seven

Seduced by The World

You adulterous people, don't you know that friendship with the world is hatred toward God? (James 4:4)

Once upon a time, a young king made a disturbing discovery. He found a newborn baby girl lying out in a field. She was a mess: naked, covered with bloody slime, her birth cord still dangling. Nobody had bothered to clean her up or put any clothing on her. Apparently she had been abandoned the moment she was born. Nobody wanted her. She had been left to die.

The king's heart ached with pity for the little one. He decided to give that filthy, helpless infant a chance to live. He picked her up in his arms, wiped her clean, wrapped her in his royal robe, and carried her to one of his estates. There, he placed her in the care of trusted friends and told them to give her an excellent upbringing and provide a superb education.

Years later, the king visited that estate and noticed that the baby he had rescued years earlier had become a lovely young woman. The king fell in love with her and asked her to marry him. She agreed, and they had a grand wedding. The king cherished his queen and lavished his riches on her. He gave her sweet perfumes, gorgeous dresses, costly jewelry, and a splendid crown. The queen became famous worldwide for her beauty. It seemed like a fairytale marriage.

But the fairy tale went bad. The queen became proud of her beauty, fine clothes, and jewelry. She got tired of her husband. She decided she could make money and enjoy herself more if she used her glamour to become a prostitute. She began selling her body to any stranger who was willing to pay, and she spent the money on wild parties. She didn't want the babies who had been born to her and the king, so she had them killed. After awhile, her beauty faded. Nobody would pay for her body anymore. So the queen started paying others to act out filthy fantasies with her.

How was the king supposed to react to all this? He had shown his wife great kindness and given her many gifts, but she had decided to seek satisfaction elsewhere. In the end, the king called her before his throne and roared,

"You adulterous wife! You prefer strangers to your own husband! Every prostitute receives a fee, but you give gifts to all your lovers, bribing them to come to you from everywhere for your illicit favors.

"Therefore, you prostitute, because you poured out your wealth and exposed your nakedness in your promiscuity with your lovers, and because you gave them your children's blood, therefore I am going to gather all your lovers, with whom you found pleasure, those you loved as well as those you hated. I will gather them against you from all around and will strip you in front of them, and they will see your nakedness. I will sentence you to the punishment of women who commit adultery and who shed blood; I will bring upon you the blood vengeance of my wrath and jealous anger. Then I will hand you over to your lovers. They will strip you of your clothes and take your fine jewelry and leave you naked and bare. They will bring a mob against you, who will stone you and hack you to pieces with swords.

"Because you did not remember the days of your youth but enraged me with all these things, I will surely bring down on your head what you have done."

God's Unfaithful Bride

That's not how a fairy tale is supposed to unfold, is it? But this is not a fairy tale. It's a story God himself tells in the Bible, in Ezekiel 16. Why would the Lord tell such a disturbing, disgusting story? God told this story to show what it's like when we forget his kindness, misuse his gifts, love other things more than we love him, and enjoy worldly pursuits rather than finding our supreme enjoyment in the Lord himself.

Originally, God spoke these words to his Old Testament people of Israel. Israel had once been a newborn nation, filthy, helpless, about to die in Egyptian slavery, with no one to help—but the Lord had loved her with tender pity and saved her from Egypt. As Israel grew and matured, she became a rich, impressive nation. The Lord loved her with the fierce passion of a husband for his wife, and he heaped blessings on her. What wondrous love! But Israel forsook her heavenly husband, went after worldly pursuits, and committed spiritual adultery by worshiping man-made idols instead of God. What hideous betrayal! God said that if Israel found other gods more attractive and wanted to give herself to the false gods of other nations, she could have them. God would hand Israel over to the cruelty of those nations and the ugliness and emptiness of their religions. Israel was invaded and carried off into exile.

Sad to say, history sometimes repeats itself. In the Old Testament, God spoke of Israel as his bride, and in the New Testament, the Lord speaks of the church as Christ's bride. But how has Christ's bride been behaving? Many of us are church members and call ourselves Christians, but how faithful have we been to our heavenly husband? All too often, our conduct has been as rotten and offensive as a cherished wife who becomes a prostitute. The Lord has gone out of his way to rescue us from ruin, he's given us all sorts of good things, but many of us have responded, not by loving him, but by becoming proud of ourselves, misusing his gifts, and seeking satisfaction in anything but God.

When we don't find our happiness and satisfaction in the Lord, we look for happiness elsewhere. Some worship sex and money, and if a baby is conceived and hampers sexual freedom or interferes with plans to make money, abortion is used to kill the baby God created. God's story about a wife-become-prostitute, who kills babies as part of her lifestyle, is right on target. In ancient Israel people were killing babies as human sacrifices to idols of sex and success, and today many people—including some who consider themselves Christians—still kill babies as part of a lifestyle where sex and success matter more than the Lord.

Spiritual Adultery

Baby-killing is often a bloody side effect of spiritual adultery, but that doesn't mean everybody who never aborted a baby or killed another person has not committed spiritual adultery. A spiritual adulterer is anyone who isn't satisfied with God and falls into the embrace of the world. A spiritual adulterer is anyone who enjoys the world's ways more than God's ways.

A spiritual adulterer would rather listen to ungodly music than sing God's praise. A spiritual adulterer would rather watch a show filled with filthy language, violence, and nudity than be entranced by the beauty of God's holiness. A spiritual adulterer would rather end an evening smirking with late-night comedians than studying Scripture. A spiritual adulterer would rather dress in showy, expensive clothing or in skimpy, seductive fashion than dress modestly as God commands. A spiritual adulterer would rather divorce a dull spouse than keep marriage promises as the Bible commands. A spiritual adulterer would rather spend hours playing golf than praying to God. A spiritual adulterer would rather spend Sunday shopping than worshipping. A spiritual adulterer would rather show off a fine house or a fancy car than boast of God's riches in Jesus Christ. A spiritual adulterer would rather play the lottery or casino than be satisfied with God's care and the fruit of hard work. A spiritual adulterer would rather sue somebody for millions than patiently endure being wronged for Christ's sake. A spiritual adulterer would rather invest more and more in stocks and bonds than invest in spreading the gospel or helping the needy. A spiritual adulterer cares more about a healthy economy than holy morality.

Spiritual adulterers would rather fit in and be approved by the world than please God. Spiritual adulterers find their greatest pleasure in the world's entertainment, the world's success, and the world's enjoyments. They live by the world's standards. The underlying reason is that their love and desire is focused on the world rather than on God.

To all such people, the Bible says in James 4:4, "You adulterous people, don't you know that friendship with the world is hatred toward God? Anyone who chooses to be a friend of the world becomes an enemy of God." Those are strong words. God doesn't just mildly suggest that worldliness might be a bit of a weakness in the way you relate to God. He says worldliness makes you an adulterer and a prostitute! The Lord doesn't say that if you're worldly, you don't love God quite as much as you should; he says you *hate* God and are his enemy. Getting cozy with the world is a fatal friendship. It's fatal to the way you relate to God, and it's fatal for your eternal soul.

The Lord tells worldly people what he told ancient Israel: "You adulterous wife! You prefer strangers to your own husband! You prostitute! You have enraged me, and I will surely bring down on your head what you have done." If you think this sounds exaggerated, keep in mind that these are the words of God himself—and God always means what he says.

So if you're not sure what it means to be worldly or why friendship with the world is fatal, you need to find out. You need your worldliness replaced with godliness, with a longing to know Jesus, to enjoy his riches and his love, and to love him with your whole being.

Undivided Loyalty

There is nothing greater than to know Christ in his death and resurrection and to live in his love forever—and there is nothing worse than to despise God's love and seek satisfaction in the world apart from God. Over and over throughout the Bible, God uses various pictures to make this point.

One picture is of working for a boss. "No servant can serve two masters," says Jesus. "Either he will hate the one and love the other, or he will be devoted to the one and despise the other. You cannot serve both God and Money" (Luke 16:13). You can't work for two competing companies and two rival bosses at the same time. You can be loyal to only one. If you work for this world, you don't work for God. In fact, you hate God.

Another way the Bible pictures this is in terms of citizenship. You can't be a loyal citizen of two different nations that are at war with each other. If you're a loyal citizen of one, you are an enemy of the other. People whose mind is on earthly things are enemies of the cross of Christ, says the apostle Paul. Their god is their appetite, and their destiny is destruction. "But," says Paul to followers of Christ, "our citizenship is in heaven" (Philippians 3:18-20).

Still another biblical picture is one we looked at earlier: marriage. You can't have a healthy marriage with your spouse and at the same time be involved in adultery and prostitution with others. In the Bible God shows himself as a tender helper and loving husband with whom we could be forever happy. He also says that loving the world instead of him is spiritual adultery and prostitution. This is one of the most powerful pictures for seeing the wonder of God's love and the horror of worldliness. "You *adulterous* people," exclaims the apostle James, "don't you know that friendship with the world is hatred toward God?"

This helps us to understand what God means when he says, "I, the Lord your God, am a jealous God" (Exodus 20:5). The fact that God is jealous doesn't mean he's petty; it means he's possessive, as any good husband is possessive. If a husband learns his wife is having an affair and smiles and says he doesn't mind, does that mean he's an excellent, loving husband? No, it means he doesn't care about her or their relationship. A truly loving husband is jealous: he refuses to share his wife with others. So too, God's love is jealous and possessive. He doesn't want us to give our hearts to anyone but him. He won't put up with spiritual adultery and prostitution. God requires undivided loyalty.

Adulterous Prayers

Sometimes, though, we think we can have it both ways. We want everything the world around us wants, but at the same time we want to maintain some sort of relationship with God. Even if we don't really love God or enjoy him, we figure we may need him in order to get some of the things we want. We don't really like listening or talking with God, but we pray anyway, in the hope that he'll give us more of the worldly things we love.

What are your prayers like? Is prayer a time first of all to enjoy the company of your Father in heaven and seek the things he wants? Or do you go to God mostly when you want something and need God's help to get it? In that case, don't be shocked if your prayers aren't answered. "When you ask, you do not receive, because you ask with wrong motives, that you may spend what you get on your pleasures" (James 4:3). Right after saying this, James goes on to say, "You adulterous people, don't you know that friendship with the world is hatred toward God?"

Of all forms of worldliness, perhaps the most disgusting to God is worldliness in prayer. What could be worse than going to God and asking him to give us the worldly things we love more than him? It's like a wife going to her husband and asking him to arrange an extramarital affair for her to enjoy or like asking a spouse for money to go out and hire a prostitute. Spiritual adultery is bad enough without praying to God for the resources to embrace the world even more than we already do.

In the Lord's prayer, Jesus taught us to pray that God's name be hallowed, that his kingdom come, that his will be done, that we live in the grace of forgiveness, that we not be led into temptation but delivered from evil. That is true prayer for someone who loves God and hates sin. As we pray for God to glorify himself and free us from sin, we may also pray for our daily bread, for enough to sustain us for another day of life. But that's a far cry from presenting God with a long wish list of worldly things we think we need to be happy, without ever seeking the glory of his name or the growth of his kingdom. It's a far cry from being so attached to this world that we pray eagerly to be spared from disease and death and find nothing attractive about leaving this world to be with Christ.

Worldliness can appear when we dress in worldly fashions or watch worldly entertainment or laugh at worldly jokes or pursue worldly wealth, but worldliness may be at its worst when we're on our knees in what we think are our most pious moments. We may be talking to heaven, but our mind is on earthly things. We don't want to talk to God about anything but our health, our finances, our success, our relationships, the big game we want to win, the good job we want to get, or whatever else in this world seems more important for our happiness than God.

You may wonder, "What's wrong with praying for God's help with day to day concerns?" Nothing—if you find your supreme happiness in God and not in those things. Many of these things aren't bad in themselves. In fact, they may be good gifts from God. But they may never replace God in our affections.

Unspectacular Worldliness

It's helpful to notice two different meanings of "the world" and two kinds of worldliness. Sometimes the Bible speaks of "the world" as a sinful system. "The world" in this sense—a group mindset of evil desires and peer pressure and rebellion against God—is something we must utterly reject and leave behind.

Sometimes, though, the Bible speaks of "the world" in a more positive way, as the earth God created and populated with living things and with people made in his image. In this sense, "the world" is something God made and upholds and loves, and it is something we should value and enjoy with thanks to God. It is a terrible blunder to take Bible verses about "the world" as a sinful system and misapply those verses to "the world" as physical creation. At times some religious people have wrongly regarded food or bodies or sex or science as evils to be frowned upon. But it is not sinful to savor a delicious meal or to delight in union with your spouse or to pursue scientific discoveries. These things are good gifts from God. However, even when we think of "the world" in this positive sense, we must beware of loving the created world more than the

Creator. Many created things aren't evil as such, but even when they're good, we can become attached to them in a way that is evil.

We need to beware of two different forms of worldliness. One kind of worldliness delights in things in this world that are by nature degrading and sinful: pornography, perversion, immodest clothing, devilish music, cruelty to competitors, violence, gambling, gossip, lying, drunkenness, and other worldly practices that are just plain sinful and wicked. Doing these things, or being entertained by such things in movies and magazines, tabloids and TV, is evil and offensive to God.

But there's another form of worldliness in which the problem isn't so much loving bad things instead of good, but loving good things instead of the best. To enjoy a lovely spouse, to work hard and earn a large income, to read a fine book or watch a thrilling drama, to be healthy and good looking—there's nothing wrong with such things in and of themselves. In fact, they are good gifts of God. But when we love created things more than the Creator, when we love the gifts more than the Giver, when we become proud of who we are and of what we have, without loving God or being thankful for his kindness, then our haughtiness and selfishness bring us into a worldliness that is just as deadly as more obvious, filthy forms of worldliness.

Don't forget God's story about the wife turned prostitute. A king rescues a helpless child, supplies her with everything to grow intelligent and beautiful, marries her, and gives her clothing, jewelry, and perfumes. What goes wrong? Is it simply that the woman in the story falls into gross adultery and prostitution and baby killing? No, that's where she eventually ends up, but the trouble begins when she trusts her beauty more than she trusts her husband (Ezekiel 16:15) and when she takes the good gifts he has given her and turns them into gods (Ezekiel 16:15-19). Her clothes, jewelry, perfume, and beauty aren't bad things.

But she forgets she owes them all to her husband, and she prizes them more than she values her husband. Only after that do her more blatant crimes occur. So too, when we love God's gifts more than we love him, we have already turned away and become his enemy, even before we fall into more obvious and outrageous sins.

In C.S. Lewis's *The Screwtape Letters*, Screwtape (a senior demon) advises Wormwood (a junior tempter) that in trying to ruin a decent, religious person, it often works best not to start by aiming for extreme evils but instead simply to get the person attached to some respectable, good things and make those things the supreme desire of his heart rather than God. Focus his prayers on earthly desires. Make him proud. Make him think the world he sees around him is all that matters. Lead him into sins that seem small, not grand and gory crimes. Screwtape tells the junior demon,

> Doubtless, like all young tempters, you are anxious to be able to report spectacular wickedness. But do remember, the only thing that matters is the extent to which you separate the man from the Enemy [God]. It does not matter how small the sins are, provided that their cumulative effect is to edge the man away from the Light and out into the Nothing. Murder is no better than cards if cards can do the trick. Indeed, the safest road to Hell is the gradual one—the gentle slope, soft underfoot, without sudden turnings, without milestones, without signposts.

The devil wants us to walk a road without signposts, love a world without standards, and end up in a hell without hope. Along the way, Satan doesn't care what we love most—as long as it's not God. Anything in this world will do.

But even as Satan tries to lead us down the broad, smooth road with no signposts, God keeps putting up signs that point us to the narrow way of Christ. When we love anything in place of him, God's voice keeps warning us,

"You adulterous people, don't you know that friendship with the world is hatred toward God? Anyone who chooses to be a friend of the world becomes an enemy of God."

Have you been committing spiritual adultery? Have you chosen a fatal friendship with the world that makes you God's enemy? Now is the time to change. Ask Jesus' forgiveness, trust his love, and love him as your supreme satisfaction.

Chapter Eight

Upsetting the World

If you belonged to the world, it would love you as its own. As it is, you do not belong to the world, but I have chosen you out of the world. That is why the world hates you. (John 15:19)

Demetrius had a problem. His business had been making big money for years, but now demand was dropping and sales were shrinking. The money was drying up.

Demetrius was the head of a company that made silver statues of a goddess called Artemis. Demetrius lived in the city of Ephesus, which had a temple for Artemis (also called Diana). Artemis was a goddess of sex and success. Her priestesses served as temple prostitutes, so if you were a man going to her temple, you could enjoy sexual encounters. When you left the temple, you could count on Artemis to give you a good sex life, a fertile family, a prosperous farm or business, and lots of fun. But you couldn't be at the temple all the time, so how could you make sure that Artemis would be near to help you when you were elsewhere? It was easy, though a bit pricey. You could buy a miniature silver statue, your personal icon of Artemis. You could take this mobile goddess with you to any location you wanted. The silver statue would be your charm for sex, prosperity, and pleasure. Selling statues of Artemis seemed like a can't-miss business, and for a long time, it was. Demetrius made big money as chairman of Artemis Incorporated, and so did many other people in related trades.

But then sales began to slump. The slump started when a stranger came to town. The stranger, named Paul, said that there was only one God and that this God had come to earth in the person of someone named Jesus. Those who believed Paul's message about Jesus stopped worshiping Artemis. They stayed away from temple prostitutes and no longer bought silver idols. That upset Demetrius. His income was going down, so he decided to take action. He held a meeting of his fellow idol makers. The meeting became a noisy protest and then a full-scale riot. The Bible tells what happened in chapter 19 of *The Acts of the Apostles*, written by a physician named Luke. I've taken Dr. Luke's account and put it into a style more like Dr. Seuss.

With a moan and a groan
and a scowl and a growl,
Demetrius snarled,
"Shall we throw in the towel?
We can't seem to sell
all these idols we've made.
The people won't buy them.
We're not getting paid."

"Our idols were selling
for oodles of money,
but now we can't sell them,
and that isn't funny.
Shall we throw in the towel?
No! I say we shall not!"
As he spoke, his friends'
tempers began to grow hot.

Then on went Demetrius,
madder than ever,
"You know who's been wrecking
our business endeavor?

This fellow named Paul!"
(All agreed with a nod.)
"This fellow keeps saying
there's only one God. "

"He says Jesus Christ
is the one all should trust.
When folks believe that,
they stop buying from us.
It's time to do something.
It can't hurt to try it.
Let's praise our great goddess
and start a great riot. "

So that's what they did,
and they did it quite well,
those furious men
with a goddess to sell.
They were stomping and shouting
and screaming so loud
that soon they attracted
an oversized crowd.

Then yelling in rage
seemed the "in" thing to do.
But why they were there,
most of them hadn't a clue.
Before long the whole town
had become one huge mob.
How to calm it back down?
An impossible job!

For two hours they screamed,
till they barely could croak.
Then the clerk of the city
stood up, and he spoke:

"What's all the commotion?
We've got a great idol.
We give her devotion.
We honor her title."

"But why attack people
who've done nothing wrong?
Why stand around squawking
so loud and so long?
This hubbub could get
our fine city in trouble.
So shut your loud mouths,
and go home on the double."

When idol-makers blow their stack
and try to start a fight,
it means God's people are on track;
we're doing something right.
But when we worship money, sex,
TVs and sports and song,
Demetrius gets filthy rich;
we're doing something wrong.

Starting An Uproar

If you read the book of Acts, you find that wherever the early Christians brought the message of Jesus, the gospel changed some people's lives in a big way and upset other people in a big way. The riot in Ephesus wasn't the first or last time there was a commotion.

Earlier, in Philippi, Paul used Jesus' authority to drive an evil spirit out of a slave girl. That angered the girl's owners, because the evil spirit had been predicting the future, and the girl's owners had made big money on fees for fortune telling.

When the owners of the slave girl realized that their hope of making money was gone, they seized Paul and Silas and dragged them into the marketplace ... and said, "These men are Jews and are throwing our city into an uproar by advocating customs unlawful for us Romans to accept or practice." The crowd joined in the attack (Acts 16:20-22). Did the apostles really push unlawful, anti-Roman behavior? No, although Paul and Silas were Jewish Christians, they were also Roman citizens and broke no Roman law. Their only "crime" was transforming a young girl's life by the power of Jesus and hurting the cash flow of those who had been exploiting the girl.

Paul and Silas next went to the city of Thessalonica and proclaimed Jesus as Messiah and Savior. Quite a few people were persuaded to become Christians, but others formed a mob and started a riot in the city.

They shouted, "These men who are turning the world upside down have now come here... They are all defying Caesar's decrees, saying that there is another king, one called Jesus." When they heard this, the crowd and the city officials were thrown into turmoil (Acts 17:5-8).

Were the apostles really defying Caesar and trying to bring down the government? No, but introducing people to Jesus as the ultimate ruler did revolutionize the way people lived. The apostles were turning the world rightside up, but to people standing on their heads, the gospel seemed upside down.

When Paul later traveled to Ephesus, the home city of Demetrius and the temple of Artemis, the pattern repeated itself: the gospel transformed some people and made others want to riot. For two years Paul stayed in Ephesus and had daily discussions about Jesus. Practically everybody in the region heard the word of the Lord. Along with the gospel teaching came healings, release from evil spirits, and other demonstrations of God's power. Response was dramatic. People revered Jesus. They openly admitted wrong things

they had done. Some even decided to have a bonfire and
burn their sorcery books. They had paid big money for
scrolls teaching them the secrets of sorcery, but now that
they belonged to Jesus, they wanted nothing to do with
sorcery. Those new Christians burned their evil books,
which had cost them a total of about 50,000 drachmas. A
drachma was a day's wage, so that was an expensive bonfire—50,000 days' wages, about 150 years of total income,
up in smoke.

It was about this time that Demetrius and his cronies
noticed that their idol-selling business wasn't doing so
well, and they blamed the recession on Paul. He was bad
for business. Paul wasn't pushing a political agenda or or-
ganizing a consumer boycott. He didn't try to pass a law
against the worship of Artemis. Still, when people got to
know Jesus, they lost interest in Artemis. Paul didn't push
for government censorship of bad books, but when people
heard the divine truths of Scripture, they knew their sorcery books were good for nothing but a bonfire. Paul didn't
push new legislation, but the Christian way of life shook
cities and societies to their foundations.

Demetrius Prospers

That brings up the question: Why were there so many
riots against Christians in that society and so few in our
society? Well, people like Demetrius don't riot if business
is good. If society remains profitable for idolatry and im-
morality, if not many people are decisively different because of the gospel, if those who claim to follow Jesus
keep buying from Demetrius, he won't get upset. In the
book of Acts, the new Christians were very different from
non-Christians around them, and Demetrius' income went
down as a result. But in our society, many church people
remain much like those without Christ, and they are as
likely as anyone else to buy from Demetrius.

If Demetrius is a Hollywood producer, does he worry about losing money because of people who follow Jesus? Not likely. When Demetrius of Hollywood produces entertainment filled with sex, slaughter, and foul language, church people are almost as likely as unchurched people to buy his theatre tickets, rent his videos, and watch his TV shows. If Demetrius runs a music company that cranks out godless, immoral albums, he can count on church teenagers to buy his garbage. Why would a modern-day Demetrius get upset at people who claim to be Christians? They are some of his best customers!

If Demetrius runs a casino, does he find that the profits from gambling are going down? No, gambling is big business and continues to expand. Growth in gambling is not just due to formerly illegal gambling being legalized, and it's not just due to non-churched people gambling more. It's also due to many church people buying lottery tickets and crowding into casinos. They are so in love with luck, so discontented with what they have, so eager for easy money, so bored with everyday work and wise stewardship of money, that they gamble away money God has entrusted to them. If Demetrius runs a casino or lottery, why would he start a riot against church people? He's too busy raking in cash from them.

If Demetrius runs a brewery, is he losing money because so many devout followers of Jesus have limited their drinking or have given up alcohol entirely? No, liquor sellers make big money, not least from churchgoers. Despite the Bible's strong words against getting drunk, many young people from churchgoing families think that getting drunk is the essence of fun. Many of their parents can't relax and have a good time unless they have several drinks to loosen things up. Many church weddings are followed by receptions with open bars, and what begins as a sacred ceremony ends as a drunken bash. If Demetrius is in the liquor business, does he object to churchgoers? Of course not. He's too busy counting the profits from their latest party.

If Demetrius runs a store that's open seven days a week, does he lose money on Sunday because so many Christians want to keep Sunday special for God and won't shop on that day? If Demetrius runs a professional sports franchise, does he have a problem because Christian players won't play on Sunday or because Christian fans stay away from the stadium on Sundays and leave their television off? No, Sunday is the number one day for pro sports, and now it's becoming a day for organized sports leagues at all levels down to youth and children. If a child has practice or a game on Sunday, and if it is scheduled at the same time as a church service—well, why not skip church? Why would Demetrius start a commotion against churchgoers when Sunday is a super moneymaker for him?

Demetrius Complains

Here and there some Christians still upset a modern-day Demetrius. If Demetrius is in politics, he doesn't mind religion if it doesn't interfere with him, but he will cause a commotion if Christians influence public policy in any significant way. Lord Melbourne of Britain was upset at a movement led by evangelical Christians, and he thundered, "Things have come to a pretty pass when religion is allowed to invade public life." What made him so angry? Those evangelical Christians were striving to end the slave trade. Slave traders would need to find a new way to make money, and the economy wouldn't profit from so much free labor. It would have been far more convenient for every slave-trading Demetrius if those Christians hadn't turned the world upside down by valuing slaves as children of God.

When Demetrius runs an abortion clinic, he is maintaining a temple for people who worship sex and money and offer human sacrifices to their goddess. He has no problem with church people who see his business as a basic right and pay him to kill their unborn babies. But he hates those who consider life sacred. Demetrius claims to be pro-choice, but he wants the choice to be death, not life. Demetrius the abortionist howls about the horror of mixing religion and politics.

If Demetrius belongs to a non-Christian religion or has no religion at all, he doesn't mind churchgoers who keep their faith to themselves. But if Christians call others to trust Jesus as Savior and Lord, and if growing numbers of people become Christians, watch out! Demetrius denounces mission-minded Christians as proselytizers and bigots, and he launches a campaign against them. Demetrius won't cause a commotion over a brand of Christianity that says almost nothing and changes almost nobody. But he'll attack Christians who live and speak in the power of Jesus and spread the Christian way to others. A dead, decaying brand of Christianity doesn't upset the world; it fits right in with the world's way of doing things. But a living, spreading faith in Jesus arouses opposition.

God-Pleaser, Not People-Pleaser

One of the chief differences between a lively Christian and a deadbeat is that the lively Christian wants God's approval, while the deadbeat cares most about the world's opinion. The apostle Paul was a God-pleaser, not a people pleaser. Paul said, "We dared to tell you his gospel in spite of strong opposition... We are not trying to please men but God" (1 Thessalonians 2:2,4). "If I were still trying to please men, I would not be a servant of Christ" (Galatians 1:10).

Some of us want to impress intellectuals. But Paul didn't fear the scorn of scholars. In Athens, the intellectual capital of the world, some philosophers disputed with Paul and asked, "What is this babbler trying to say?" When Paul spoke about the resurrection of the dead, some of them sneered at him (Acts 17). But Paul spoke the gospel clearly, despite the mockery of many intellectuals, and some became Christians as a result. Why be intimidated by what intellectuals say about you? The Bible says that intellectuals in Athens "spent their time doing nothing but talking about and listening to the latest ideas" (Acts 17:21). Many in our universities do the same thing. They have lectures and debates without end, but they have no grasp of the basic truths that give life meaning and direction. If they have no convictions about the things that matter most, why be intimidated if they sneer at your beliefs?

Don't fear the jeers of intellectuals, and don't worry about public opinion. In the riot at Ephesus led by Demetrius, a huge mob gathered in the temple of Artemis and yelled at the top of their lungs for two hours. It may have looked like an impressive demonstration, and if such a commotion took place today, it would certainly be featured on the TV news. But the Bible says of these noisy, showy demonstrators, "Most of them did not even know why they were there" (Acts 19:32). They were upset because—well, just because everybody else was upset. Being upset was the thing to do. That's how it is with public opinion and noisy crowds. A few cunning ringleaders (like Demetrius) have an agenda, but many others join the commotion without even knowing why they are there. So let's not be too upset if we don't fit into the mainstream of public opinion or if we feel outnumbered. God's evaluation is what matters.

Paul couldn't afford to take people's opinions too seriously. Some people differed wildly from others, and even the same people could swing from one extreme to another in a short time. In one city, Lystra, Paul used the power of Christ to heal a man who had been crippled all his life because of a birth defect. When the man jumped up and began to walk, the crowd shouted, "The gods have come down to us in human form." But a short time later, that same crowd turned against Paul and pelted him with rocks in an effort to kill him (Acts 14:8-20). One minute Paul was a god, the next minute he wasn't fit to live.

On another occasion, Paul was gathering wood for a fire when a poisonous snake bit him. A crowd of people nearby thought Paul must be a murderer and this was the divine death penalty for his crime. "But Paul shook the snake into the fire and suffered no ill effects. The people expected him to swell up or suddenly fall dead, but after waiting a long time and seeing nothing unusual happen to him, they changed their minds and said he was a god" (Acts 28:5-6). A criminal one moment, a god the next—when people's opinions swing between such extremes, it's far better not to worry what they think of you. Just focus on God's evaluation of you.

In one of the many riots that broke out in reaction to Paul's ministry, an officer asked him, "Aren't you the Egyptian who started a revolt and led four thousand terrorists out into the desert some time ago?" (Acts 21:38) The commander was surprised to learn that Paul spoke his language and was a fellow citizen who had nothing to do with foreign terrorists.

You never know what rumors might spread about you or what people might think of you, and that's all the more reason to focus on what God thinks of you. The early Christians were rumored to be terrorists, rumored to be atheists, rumored to be arsonists who set Rome on fire, rumored to be cannibals, rumored to be all sorts of horrible things, but the rumors were false. They were simply followers of Jesus who upset the world by trusting Jesus, living for Jesus, and calling others to Jesus. Still today, if you are a Christian worth your salt, some people will despise and oppose you, but your goal is not to be a people pleaser but a God-pleaser. You have one commander, not many. His name is Jesus.

Badge of Honor

If Christians are accused of stirring up trouble, it's not necessarily a disgrace. It may be a huge honor. Jesus says, "If the world hates you, keep in mind that it hated me first. If you belonged to the world, it would love you as its own. As it is, you do not belong to the world, but I have chosen you out of the world. That is why the world hates you... If they persecuted me, they will persecute you also" (John 15:18-20). Religion that suits the world is out of touch with Jesus. If it never provokes opposition, it won't provide salvation.

The only kind of Christianity worth joining is the kind that's worth opposing. If churches offer religion that is so weak or so worldly that idol worshipers don't feel any need to oppose it, then it's not worth joining by those who seek the living God. This doesn't mean Christians are eager to make enemies. It simply means that a faithful Christian life and witness will unavoidably upset the world. It will provoke hostility from those who prefer life without Christ and who, like Demetrius, feel they have too much to lose if Christianity spreads too much. A gospel that never turns anybody off will probably not turn anybody on to the reality of salvation in Jesus and the revolutionary new life that comes from his Holy Spirit and is taught in the Holy Bible.

There's one thing I don't want you to miss in all this: the huge joy and privilege of serving Jesus. Why do you think Paul was willing to face so much misunderstanding? Why didn't he just stay home and keep quiet and not stir things up? Why do you think he kept telling people about Jesus, despite rumors, riots, beatings, and attempts to kill him? Because none of these problems mattered compared to knowing Jesus and having a relationship with him. Paul wanted to follow Jesus and stay close to him, no matter what the cost, because he had tasted the Lord's goodness. He knew that the benefit was so huge it would always outweigh the cost. Paul wanted to bring others to Jesus so that they too could enjoy what he already enjoyed: a transformed life now and eternal life with Christ in the future.

Many people outside the church have never tasted the joy of Jesus, and even many in the church have a wimpy, worthless religion. They don't upset the world; they are just like the world. They have none of the thrilling, life-changing power of the Holy Spirit. The church needs a revival of power and a renewal of holiness so that the impact of Christ will be impossible to ignore.

When that happens, Demetrius and his pals may be eager to start a riot, but many others will leave behind the emptiness of the sinful world for fullness in Christ. They will turn away from the goddess of sex and success. They will stop buying into lies. They will believe the truth and receive the free gift of eternal life in Jesus. Many people inside the church may discover for the first time the Lord they have always claimed to believe in, and many outside the church will get to know Jesus and become part of his living church. The world will be upset, but God's people will be uplifted.

Chapter Nine

Fighting the Flesh

I do not do the good I want to do, but the evil I do not want to do—this I keep on doing. (Romans 7:19)

For the flesh desires what is contrary to the Spirit, and the Spirit what is contrary to the flesh. They are in conflict with each other. (Galatians 5:17)

Phil sits in front of his computer. His hand hovers over the mouse, hesitating. Then he clicks it. Soon the screen is showing him one dirty picture after another. Phil feels ashamed about looking at pornography, and he tells himself he should shut the computer off. But even as he tells himself this, he clicks the mouse and looks at some more dirty pictures. Something in him doesn't want to do it, but something else in him does it anyway.

Jennifer is a teenager. At breakfast her dad asks, "Where'd you go last night, Jen?" Jennifer hates lying, but how can she tell the truth? Last night she was out smoking pot with some of her friends. So for the umpteenth time Jennifer makes up a story and lies about where she was. Her dad's eyes narrow a bit, wondering, but he doesn't push the matter. Something in Jennifer doesn't really want to smoke pot with her friends or lie to her dad, but something else in her does it anyway.

George just got home from work. It's been a tough day. He asks his wife, "What's for dinner?" She says they'll be having leftovers. "Leftovers!" George shouts. "I work like a dog all day, and the only thing I get is leftovers from that lousy meal we had last night? Why can't you give me some decent food?" George snarls a few swear words and then notices his wife's lip quivering and a tear trickling down her cheek. George shuts his mouth and sits down. He really does care about his wife, but this isn't the first time he's lost his temper and yelled at her. Something in George doesn't want to blow up, but something else in him does it anyway.

Amy has been on the phone for quite awhile. She has been drinking in all the latest gossip from her friend, and she adds several gallons of her own juicy gossip to the grapevine. After she hangs up the phone, she hangs her head. Some of what she said was unkind. Although some of it was true, she didn't have to repeat it. Amy knows that she gossips too much, and she knows it would be better not to spread hurtful talk. Something in her doesn't want to do it, but something else in her does it anyway.

Maybe you have your own habit or pattern of behavior that's bad for you or just plain wrong. Something in you wants to be different, but something else makes you keep doing the same old thing, and you wonder, "What's wrong with me? I know what's good, and yet I keep doing what's bad. Why do I have this war going on inside me, and why does the bad side seem to keep winning?"

The Bible describes this predicament in Romans 7. When we hear God's law in Scripture or sense God's will in our own conscience, we might see that God's way is best. But even if we agree with God's law, we often do the opposite. In Romans 7:14-20 the apostle Paul says,

We know that the law is spiritual; but I am unspiritual, sold as a slave to sin. I do not understand what I do. For what I want to do I do not do, but what I hate I do. And if I do what I do not want to do, I agree that the law is good. As it is, it is no longer I myself who do it, but it is sin living in me.

I know that nothing good lives in me, that is, in my
sinful nature. For I have the desire to do what is
good, but I cannot carry it out. For what I do is not
the good I want to do; no, the evil I do not want to
do—this I keep on doing. Now if I do what I do not
want to do, it is no longer I who do it, but it is sin
living in me that does it.

What a tangle! When I'm caught between God's will and
my own sinful tendencies, I don't understand what I do,
and I don't understand who I am. I do bad things—but is it
really I, or is it an alien power of sin living in me? Nothing
good lives in me—in my sinful nature, that is—and yet
something in me affirms and even likes what is truly spiritual and good. Who am I anyway? Is my real self the one
that agrees with God's law, or is my real self the one that
keeps breaking God's law? Am I two different persons?
Do I have a split personality? Why can't I control my conduct or figure out who I really am? What's this war within?

Those are questions you may find yourself asking
when you keep doing things you'd rather not do. Whether
it's pornography or a drinking problem or drug use or lying
or a hot temper or homosexual activity or gossip or whatever, when you're driven to do things your conscience
condemns, you ask yourself, "What makes me go against
my own better judgment? Am I to blame? Can I be forgiv-
en? Can I ever be different? Is there any way out?"

Paul ends Romans 7 by talking about this war within
and telling the only way to win it. He says,

So I find this law at work: When I want to do good,
evil is right there with me. For in my inner being I
delight in God's law; but I see another law at work
in the members of my body, waging war against the
law of my mind and making me a prisoner of the
law of sin at work within my members. What a
wretched man I am! Who will rescue me from this

body of death? Thanks be to God—through Jesus Christ our Lord!

No matter how wretched we are, no matter what's wrong with us, the Lord can forgive, rescue, and change us.

The Sinful Nature

We desperately need God to forgive us and change us. Before we explore how that happens, let's probe a bit further into our core problem. We have a fallen self that is against God, is allergic to God, and reacts against his holy law. The Bible calls this "the flesh" or "the sinful nature."

Bible-believing Christians speak of three threats to a person's spiritual and eternal wellbeing: the devil, the world, and the flesh. That's a deadly trio. The devil, Satan, is strong and sneaky. The world can corrupt us and seduce us away from God. But the devil and the world aren't our only enemies. There's also the flesh, our own sinful nature. When we do something wrong, we can't just say, "The devil made me do it!" or blame it on the world around us. We have to admit that right inside us is a sinful nature that is all too quick to follow the devil, fall in love with the world, and war against what we know to be right.

This sinful nature is called "the flesh" in many Bible translations and other Christian writings. Don't be confused by this term. Don't think that "the flesh" refers only to sins of the body, like sexual sin or gluttony. "The flesh" means the entire self—body, soul, mind, and emotions—in the grip of sin. "The flesh" is the whole tangle of ungodly cravings and thoughts and habits of our entire fallen self.

Whether we call it "the flesh" or "the sinful nature," we have to face the reality of it. When we find ourselves doing things we know are wrong, we might want to say, "Oh, I just made a mistake," or "I could change that any time I want" or "I'm basically a good person; I just happen to slip once in awhile." But if we're realistic, we have to say with the biblical writer, "I am unspiritual, sold as a slave to sin.

I know that nothing good lives in me, that is, in my sinful nature."

When the flesh, the sinful nature, is confronted by God's law, the result isn't pleasant. The law tells us what we should be doing and condemns us when we don't do it, but God's law doesn't change our sinful nature. In fact, sometimes being told what's right just stirs up more of what's wrong inside us. The more we're told not to do something, the more our sinful nature reacts by doing the opposite. And if we feel guilty about it, our guilt feelings may actually drive us to do it even more. Strange as it sounds, it's true. The more we know God's law and sense that it's right, the more wretched we become.

Surrender to Sin

The war within is so hard, so painful, that we want it to end. One tempting way of ending the struggle is to surrender to sin. This can seem appealing, especially if you've been fighting hard with little sign of progress. A young man had homosexual cravings that wouldn't go away. He fought these feelings, and for a while he believed that God was against homosexual acts. But when he couldn't change his desires, eventually he concluded it was okay to have a gay partner. He also convinced his parents of this, even though they had formerly thought homosexual behavior was wrong. If their son couldn't change, God must not want him to change. His mother said, "God created my son gay for a reason, and he's not out of his will."

Such thinking is common among people from a religious background who are involved in homosexual activity. Regarding their same-sex tendency, they say, "I didn't choose it, and I can't change it, so that means I was born with it. If I was born with it, then God made me this way. And if God made me this way, then my homosexual craving is a beautiful thing to express and enjoy, not a sin to regret and repent of and struggle against."

Sounds pretty convincing, doesn't it? But the reason it sounds convincing is that so few of us think in terms of the biblical understanding of sin. When I mention the biblical understanding of sin, I'm not just talking about biblical commands against homosexual behavior. The deeper problem is the underlying assumption that any strong tendency ingrained in my nature, anything I'm born with, must be created by God and, therefore, good. That's totally at odds with the biblical teaching about our sinful nature. It's true that God created humanity good, but Adam and Eve fell into sin, and now every new member of the human race is born with a sinful nature. When God showed biblical writers the truth about themselves, what did they say? "Surely I was sinful at birth" (Psalm 51:5). "I know that nothing good lives in me, that is, in my sinful nature... What a wretched man I am" (Romans 7:18).

Arguing "I was born that way" to show something is okay would not convince anyone who knows the Bible and knows we're all born with a sinful nature. But if we assume we're born good, then whatever seems to come naturally can't be wrong. Instead of crying, "What a wretched man I am! Who will deliver me?" we announce, "This is the way I am, and I'm proud of it! Don't anyone try to change me."

If we experience a war within where our sinful nature fights against God's will, we might try to convince ourselves that the Bible is wrong, or that God can't possibly mean what he seems to be saying, or that it simply doesn't apply to our situation. We can't bear to believe that anything deeply ingrained in us can be totally at odds with what is right and good. If we were born a certain way, or if we have a cluster of feelings and a pattern of behavior that we've tried to change without success, it's a relief to surrender, to tell ourselves we're fine the way we are and we really shouldn't want to change, after all. But if we take that approach, we're lying to ourselves.

Surrender to Christ

If we are realistic, we will see the truth and goodness of God's law, and at the same time we will see that our behavior is wrong and rises out of a sinful nature that all our efforts can't change. This is painful to accept, and it's even worse because we can't fix the problem ourselves. All we can do is give up and wonder in desperation if someone else might be able to help us.

If you have a bad temper and can't change, don't pretend it's not so bad to be a hothead. If you keep looking at dirty pictures and videos, don't pretend it's okay to see other humans as objects of your lust. If you misuse alcohol, stop telling yourself you can handle your liquor. If you're in the habit of lying whenever it seems convenient, don't pretend it's no big deal. If you gossip rather than building others up, don't pretend it's harmless. Let the sad truth sink in: God's law is spiritual, but you are unspiritual. Nothing good lives in you, that is, in your sinful nature.

I know it's no fun to hear this. I was once asked to speak at a convention of young adults. The people who invited me wanted me to speak about the holiness of God. "But," they said, "do it in a way that won't make people feel guilty." How was I supposed to do that? How can people sense the holiness of God without feeling guilty? When Isaiah saw God's holiness, he cried, "Woe to me! I am ruined!" When Paul considered God's holy law, he groaned, "What a wretched man I am! Who will rescue me?"

Let's not be so eager to avoid feeling bad. You're far closer to God's kingdom if you're miserable and frustrated in your struggle with sin than if you've surrendered to sin and think there's nothing wrong with you. If you have a drinking problem but think you don't have a problem, you won't feel as miserable as the person who admits he's an alcoholic but hasn't yet found a way to stop drinking. But the miserable person is closer to reality and more likely to seek help outside himself. Before you can be free from what's wrong with you, you first have to admit that something *is* wrong and that you're powerless to change it.

One of the great purposes of God's law is to bring us to that point. The law can't forgive us or transform us, but God's law can show us our predicament and make us give up on ourselves and prepare us to depend entirely on the Lord Jesus Christ.

Watchman Nee, a Chinese Christian leader from an earlier generation, told of a man in deep water who wasn't able to swim. However, there was an expert swimmer nearby. As Nee watched, he expected this man to rescue the other one immediately. But he did nothing. "Don't you see he's drowning?" shouted Nee. But still the good swimmer did nothing. Meanwhile, the drowning man grew weaker and fainter. Nee thought to himself, "How awful that this great swimmer won't rescue a drowning brother." But just as the drowning man ran out of energy and stopped thrashing around, the swimmer sped to him in a few swift strokes, took hold of him, and brought him safely to shore. Nee scolded the swimmer for waiting so long, but the man replied, "Any earlier, and he would have pulled me under with him. A drowning man cannot be rescued until he is utterly exhausted and stops trying to save himself."

So too, when you and I are drowning in sin, the Lord may let us thrash around for awhile, trying desperately to save ourselves and change our ways. Of course God is not worried that we could pull him under, but he knows that before we are rescued, we must first give up any hope of earning the right to heaven or making ourselves holy on our own. God's holy law leaves us exhausted and helpless before the face of God. If our only hope of holiness and heaven were our ability to do the good things commanded in God's law, we would be ruined.

But just when we give up and cry, "Who will deliver me?" we may find ourselves saying, "Thanks be to God— through Jesus Christ our Lord! Therefore there is now no condemnation for those who are in Christ Jesus, because through Christ Jesus the law of the Spirit of life set me free from the law of sin and death" (Romans 8:1-2).

Jesus' death pays for all the times we've broken God's law despite knowing better, so we don't have to be weighed down by guilt. Jesus died for us—and we also die with him. Our sinful nature is crucified with Christ, and God raises up a new nature within us that is alive with the life of the risen Christ. Jesus' life-giving Holy Spirit transforms us and makes us truly ourselves for the first time. The Holy Spirit has power far greater than the sinful flesh within us, far greater than the power of Satan and the world around us. The Holy Spirit's power transforms us in a way that our own efforts never could. Fighting the flesh by his power, we can win the war within.

Without the Holy Spirit, you can't win the war within. If you're caught in a war between your conscience and your sinful nature, the sinful nature will win the war. Conscience may say that God's law is right and that sin is wrong, but conscience does not empower us to do right. The longer the war goes on, the less conscience fights. The more we sin, the more confused our conscience becomes, and the less it tries to be heard.

The Holy Spirit does what conscience cannot do. The Holy Spirit doesn't just tell us that God's law is right; the Holy Spirit encourages and empowers us to do right. The Holy Spirit is stronger than the sinful nature. The Spirit and the sinful nature fight against one another, but the Spirit is stronger. The Bible tells Spirit-filled believers, "You, however, are not controlled by the sinful nature but by the Spirit, if the Spirit of God lives in you" (Romans 8:9).

The True You

Does this mean that you become instantly perfect and free from sin the moment the Spirit of God moves in? No, as long as we're in this life, there will still be times even for born again Christians when the sinful nature acts up—like a body that's dead but still twitching. Whenever the sinful nature does that, it must be nailed back down to the cross. When you're in Christ, your old sinful nature is killed, and it must stay dead. Crucifying the old nature isn't a matter of hating yourself. It's a matter of hating a sinful nature which is not the true self God designed you to be. When you sin, don't say, "That's just who I am." Say instead, "That's not the real me; it's sin dwelling in me—and by God's grace, sin is not going to have the upper hand." Count on Christ to forgive your failure, and nail that sinful nature to his cross more firmly than ever. Then depend on the Holy Spirit to keep changing you, until one day you're holy like Christ himself and at home with him in heaven.

To win the war within, you must depend on the Holy Spirit, not on your own will power. It's like flying. If you want to fly, what should you do? Well, you can tape some feathers to your arms and legs and flap them as hard as you can, but you'll never get off the ground that way. All your feathers and flapping can't overcome the law of gravity. But if you get into an airplane, the law of aerodynamics will overcome the law of gravity for you. You can't fly on your own, but if you're in the airplane, you fly as the plane flies.

So too, if you want to soar higher morally and spiritually, you can try as hard as you want, but none of your efforts can overcome the weight of your fallen flesh, your sinful nature. But if you are in Christ by faith, the power of the Spirit of Christ overcomes the weight of sin and lifts you to a higher level in Christ. The Bible says, "What the law was powerless to do ... God did!" (Romans 8:3).

If you've been trying to do good but have kept doing bad instead, if you believe God's law is holy but haven't been able to keep it, then give up on yourself, and go to Christ. He will not condemn you. He will forgive and welcome you. Accept his forgiveness, and then trust him to help you to make the changes you cannot make on your own. Depend on his Holy Spirit for the power to fight the flesh. Get together with a group of other Christ-believing, Spirit-empowered people who have been through the same struggle you've been through, who know the addictive, enslaving power of the sinful nature but also know the joyous liberating power of God. When you live in the forgiveness of Christ, in the power of his Spirit, and in the encouragement and accountability of God's people, your sinful nature will give way to the new, true you. Pray each day for fresh strength from the Holy Spirit. A centuries-old prayer in the Heidelberg Catechism provides guidance for praying against evil:

Father in heaven, deliver us from evil. By ourselves we are too weak to hold our own even for a moment. And our sworn enemies—the devil, the world, and our own flesh—never stop attacking us. And so, Lord, uphold us and make us strong with the strength of your Holy Spirit, so that we may not go down in defeat in this spiritual struggle, but may firmly resist our enemies until we finally win the complete victory, through Jesus Christ our Lord.

Part Three

Combat Equipment:
The Armor of God

Therefore put on the full armor of God, so that when the day of evil comes, you may be able to stand your ground.

(Ephesians 6:13)

The weapons we fight with are not the weapons of the world. On the contrary, they have divine power to demolish strongholds.

(2 Corinthians 10:4)

We are more than conquerors through him who loved us.

(Romans 8:37)

The one who conquers, I will grant him to sit with me on my throne.

(Revelation 3:21)

Chapter Ten

The Belt of Truth

Stand firm, then, with the belt of truth buckled around your waist. (Ephesians 6:14)

Nothing, it seemed, could kill George Washington. As a young man, Washington caught smallpox but survived the dreaded disease and remained as strong and athletic as ever. As a junior officer, Washington was part of a unit that was caught in an ambush. His commanding general and most of his fellow soldiers were shot down. Washington had two horses shot from under him and four bullet holes in his coat, but not one bullet touched his body. Later, as general during the American war for independence, Washington would ride his horse where fighting was fiercest, with bullets and cannon fire whistling all around him, but he was not hit. He camped with troops in awful conditions, with many men dying of disease, but Washington survived it all.

Nothing could kill George Washington—except his doctors. After Washington retired from the presidency, he was riding his horse in the rain one day and caught a cold and sore throat. His throat got sore and swollen, so his doctors tried to help him. The doctors shared the medical opinion common at the time that one good way to get rid of a disease was to bleed it out. It was thought that when diseased blood was drained from someone, the body would replace it with fresh, healthy blood in a short time. So a pint of blood was drained from Washington. A bit later another pint was drained, and shortly after that, still another pint. When Washington didn't improve, the doctors decided they should bleed him again, and this time they took a full quart of blood rather than just a pint. The doctors also used other methods to drain the disease. They gave Washington laxatives to drain his bowels. They gave him vomit-inducing drugs to drain his stomach. They blistered his hands and feet to release disease through the skin. They did all this in addition to draining five pints of his blood. At last the doctors drained all the life out of him, and George Washington died.

The treatments he received were not based on truth. Truth is vital in medicine, and truth is vital in all of life. Error in the medical realm killed George Washington, and error in the spiritual realm destroys souls. Nice intentions aren't enough; there must be truth. Falsehood destroys; truth protects and strengthens.

You may like to think that every religion is as helpful as any other, but that's like saying every medical treatment is as helpful as any other. Is draining five pints of blood from an infected person as helpful as giving that person antibiotics? No, treatment must be based on truth, or it does more harm than good. Likewise, religion must be grounded in truth, or it does more harm than good. Doctrinal errors are even deadlier than doctors' errors. False religion can destroy you for eternity.

Maybe you'd rather not distinguish truth from error. You may think it doesn't matter what you believe as long as you're sincere about it. Well, George Washington's doctors were very sincere. They sincerely cared about Washington and sincerely thought they were taking the best approach to healing him. Washington sincerely trusted his doctors and gave his consent at every step of the treatment. But no matter how sincere they were, their approach was based on error, not truth. Error killed Washington, and error can destroy you. You need truth in order to connect with God and enjoy eternal life.

When the Bible describes the armor of God that protects people from Satan and hell, the first item mentioned is "the belt of truth." Ephesians 6:14 says, "Stand firm then, with the belt of truth buckled around your waist." A belt might seem unimportant compared to such things as a breastplate, helmet, shield, or sword. But at the time this Bible passage was written, a soldier would buckle his belt firmly in place before putting on any other armor or weapons. It was the very first piece of armor the soldier would put on. The belt was a wide, tough girdle that helped protect the softer parts of the lower body. It was important in its own right for protection, and it was also needed to hold other equipment in place. The breastplate was attached to the belt, and the sword was also attached to the belt. The soldier needed his belt on before he could put on other equipment. In the armor of God, truth is the belt. What a belt did for soldiers of long ago, truth does for soldiers of Christ. It protects parts of us that are vulnerable, and it keeps other God-given equipment in place.

Protecting Soft Spots

How does truth protect us? The belt of truth helps protect parts of us that are softest and most vulnerable to wounds from Satan. We shouldn't press the details of a word picture too far, but it may be worth noting the location of a soldier's belt/girdle: near the stomach and private parts. Few appetites are as strong as the desires for food and sex. If any part of us needs to be bound and protected by truth, it is here. Without the protection of truth, our stomach is vulnerable to gluttony or to the sense that material things are all that matter. The belt of biblical truth protects us by warning against letting our stomach be our god (Philippians 3:19) and by telling us what Jesus told Satan, "Man does not live on bread alone but on every word that comes from the mouth of God" (Matthew 4:4). Without the belt of truth, our sexuality is vulnerable to promiscuous, perverted desires. But the belt of biblical truth warns against adultery, fornication, homosexuality, and other sinful distortions, and the belt of biblical truth also shows us God's beautiful design for the union of husband and wife.

But let's not limit the belt of biblical truth to the area of a physical belt, such as stomach and sexuality. Truth is vital in every area. Truth tells us that we have an eternal future, and this protects us from the deadly lie that this life is all there is. Truth tells us who God really is and what he's really like, protecting us from idols and false gods. Truth tells us who we are as creatures made in God's image and as fallen into sin, protecting us from having too low an opinion of our value and too high an opinion of our virtue. Truth shows us ultimate reality in Jesus, protecting us from putting anything else on the throne of our hearts. Truth is vital in every area, and error is deadly. Indeed, the difference between truth and lies is the difference between God and Satan. Scripture speaks of the Lord as "the God of truth" (Isaiah 65:16) and of Satan as "the father of lies" (John 8:44). Satan uses error to attack us; God uses truth to protect us.

Of all the sins and errors that can harm us, none is worse than errors about what it takes to save us. Various religions offer different ways of salvation, but only the blood of Jesus can bring pardon for our guilt, and only the divine life of Jesus can give us eternal life. That is the truth. Religions that ignore or deny this truth may offer other cures, but these cures kill. No sin is as deadly as a false way of salvation. Some cures are worse than the disease they are supposed to heal. George Washington's sore throat may have been serious, but his doctors' attempts to help him were even worse. Likewise, sin is serious, but false religions and phony ways of salvation are deadlier than any particular sin. Truth is a belt of protection against false ways of salvation and against all Satan's lies. The way to buckle truth in place is to believe with all our heart the vital truths God reveals in the Bible.

Holding Things in Place

A soldier's belt was the first piece of armor he put on. It was important for helping to protect the lower part of the torso, and it was also important for holding other equipment in place, such as the breastplate and the sword. In the armor of God, the belt of truth holds other things in place. The breastplate of righteousness can stay in place only when it's connected to the belt of truth. The sword of the Spirit, God's Word, will be available as a weapon only when the belt of truth keeps it close to our side.

Regarding the breastplate of righteousness: righteousness is having a right standing with God by measuring up to God's perfect character. The only human who measures up perfectly is the God-man, Jesus Christ. The only way I can have God's righteousness is by having Jesus' perfection credited to me as a gift. I can't make my own breastplate of righteousness. Jesus makes a breastplate of *his* righteousness and gives it to me. The way I put it on is by faith, by trusting that Jesus' perfection counts as mine. This breastplate protects my heart from Satan's accusations that I am unrighteous and unacceptable to God. This breastplate repels every stab of guilt and despair.

What does the breastplate of righteousness have to do with the belt of truth? Well, just as a soldier couldn't put on the breastplate without first putting on the belt and connecting the breastplate to it, so I can't receive God-given righteousness unless I first believe God-revealed truth. I must believe that God speaks the truth and keeps his promises before I can receive his promised gift of righteousness in Christ. Scripture says Christ is the righteousness of God for those who believe. Is that true, or isn't it? If I don't have confidence in God's Word and don't believe it's true,

I can't possibly receive that righteousness for myself. But if I first get buckled up in God's truth and take him at his word, his righteousness connects with his truth and covers me. No one ever received righteousness in Christ without believing the truth about Christ.

The belt of truth provides a connection to help hold the breastplate of righteousness in place, and the belt of truth also keeps the sword of the Spirit at hand for immediate use. The sword of the Spirit is the Word of God. God's Word, given to us in the Bible, is the chief weapon in fighting spiritual battles. But a sword is of little value to us if it's not at our side when we need it most, and the Bible is of little value to us if it's just lying around somewhere, but is not belted at our side by our love of truth and confidence in truth. If we belt on God's truth by believing the Scriptures and studying God's revelation and storing it in our minds, then we also have God's Word near at hand as a weapon when we need to fight.

We shouldn't stretch a word picture too far. In a sense we could say that the belt of truth and the sword of the Spirit are the very same thing: God's Word, the Bible. The main point is to depend on Scripture. Still, before we can put the Bible to use in daily living and in winning others to Christ, we must first know it and have biblical truth buckled around our being.

Wearing the Belt

Are you wearing the belt of truth? Are you convinced that the Bible is God's truth? Do you believe that Scripture is the message of the Lord who cannot lie? How often do you read the Bible? How well do you know it? How much of it do you memorize? How eagerly do you listen to biblical preaching? How often do you study the Bible with others? Do you take knowledge of the truth with you wherever you go and in whatever you do? Are you wrapped firmly in the belt of truth? Do you count on God's truth in Christ to keep other things in place?

Truth is vital, and so much else depends on it. Buckle it on! Wear it! If a belt was left hanging on a hook or off in a corner somewhere, it wouldn't help a soldier much, and other pieces of armor won't be of much use either, because the belt helped keep things in place. Likewise, a Bible gathering dust on a shelf somewhere is of little use in battling Satan. You need God's truth for its own sake, and you need the truth so that God's other blessings can be in place. You need the truth!

Truth is the basis for lasting success. If you want to succeed as an auto mechanic, you must learn the truth about cars. If you want to succeed as an architect, you must learn the truth about construction design. If you want to succeed as a history teacher, you must learn the truth about history. If you want to succeed as a surgeon, you must learn the truth about anatomy. If you want to succeed as a pilot, you must learn the truth about operating an airplane. In one area of life after another, success depends on knowing the truth. This is supremely true in relating to God and succeeding as part of the armies of Christ.

I would not want to live in a house designed by an architect who didn't know any principles of safe construction. I would not want to be operated on by a surgeon who knew nothing about the inner workings of the body. I would not want to get on an airplane with a pilot who didn't know how to fly. And I would not want my eternal life to depend on someone who doesn't know God or the way to God. For eternal life, I depend on Jesus himself as the way, the truth, and the life. As I live by faith in Jesus and as I teach others, I want to base everything on the teaching of Jesus and have as much of the mind of Christ as I possibly can. I can't afford to be careless about truth, and neither can you. Truth is crucial for your eternal future and for the future of those whom you influence—children, friends, neighbors, fellow workers. You can't be saved without truth, and you can't help others be saved without truth.

Belonging to a religious group is no substitute for knowing truth personally and buckling the belt of truth firmly in place. If you don't know the truth personally, you may never notice if the religious group you belong to has no real truth. If you don't have a deep love of truth, if you aren't constantly seeking to gain more truth and to understand it better, you may lose what little truth you had and not even know it.

William Gurnall, a Christian from centuries ago, wrote a classic titled *The Christian in Complete Armor*, which has been helpful for my own life and helpful in writing about spiritual warfare. Gurnall said,

> If we do not desire to know truth we have already rejected it… Truth and error are all the same to the ignorant man and so he calls everything truth. Have you heard about the covetous man who constantly hugged his bags of gold? He never opened them or used the treasure, and thus when a thief stole the gold and left his bags full of pebbles in his room, he was as happy as when he still had the gold.

That's what can happen if you belong to a religious group but never bother to check whether it's actually teaching the truth. When people stop studying the Scriptures and stop seeking God's truth, they hardly know the difference if the truth is stolen from their church by false teachers. As long as the show goes on in some form, they never realize that the jewels of truth have been taken away and replaced by rocks of worthless error, and they will have no treasure in heaven. Belonging to a religious group is no substitute for seeking the truth personally. You must know biblical truth for yourself.

Community of Truth

Does this mean the search for truth is entirely personal and private, and that you should ignore the community of faith? No, just because a soldier is responsible to put on the belt of truth doesn't mean he's an army by himself and can ignore everyone else. It may be heroic for a soldier to arm himself well and to do his part bravely, but it would be foolish for a soldier to always stay separate from fellow soldiers. Christ calls his soldiers not to remain alone but to stand together with each other in the truth. Love of truth must be personal but not merely private. Those who love truth are eager to learn from other seekers of truth and to band together with them.

There are false, misguided religious groups out there, including some that claim to be churches of the Lord. You must know biblical truth well enough to recognize when a church has fallen into deadly error, and you should stay away from such a group. But don't use the error of some as an excuse to avoid all churches. There are many congregations that truly exalt Jesus and teach the truth of the Bible. Such congregations are part of the great church that extends throughout all history and on every continent, what the Bible calls "the church of the living God, the pillar and foundation of the truth" (1 Timothy 3:15). The true church is a mighty fortress of truth, and Satan's forces will never conquer it. Jesus promises, "I will build my church; and the gates of hell shall not prevail against it" (Matthew 16:18). Don't fall for the lie that all congregations are too corrupt for you to join. The true church still stands, the gates of hell shall not prevail against it, and every soldier of Christ should be connected to a congregation if possible.

At various times in history, Satan has peddled the lie that no true church is left, and he peddles the same lie still today. Satan believes in recycling. The lies that fool people in one era of history, Satan recycles in a slightly different form for another era. The anti-church lie is a favorite in Satan's recycling operation.

A religious radio broadcaster named Harold Camping made the news by wrongly predicting the date of Jesus' return. But that wasn't Camping's biggest error. He also declared that the church age had ended and that Christians should stay away from anything that called itself a church. Camping said that God had no further use for the church and that God worked only through non-church ways, such as Camping's radio network. Harold Camping quoted the Bible a lot, but in saying that no church was worth joining, he was recycling a very old lie of Satan. Camping was very sincere—as sincere as George Washington's doctors who bled him to death in an effort to cure him. Many people are already too isolated, too dependent on their own limited wisdom, too removed from the shared wisdom and encouragement of people who know the Bible and love the Lord. Telling people to become Christians but to avoid churches is like telling them to join the army but stay away from other soldiers.

Not all churches teach the exact same thing on every point. Maybe you're tempted to think that if they can't agree on every point, you're not going to join any of them. But don't make too much of minor differences among Bible-believing Christians who agree on the basic truths of what God is like, of human nature, of salvation through God's grace in Christ, and of Christian moral principles. If you really love truth, don't let disagreements about smaller truths get in the way of the fact that many churches agree on the really big truths.

If you refuse to join any church because churches aren't all exactly alike and don't entirely agree on every exact point, says William Gurnall, you are "as foolish as the man who refused to eat his noon meal until all clocks in the city struck twelve at exactly the same time." Think of it: noontime arrives, and various clocks start chiming, but they're a few seconds apart from each other. They don't quite chime in perfect unison. Is that a good reason to deny that it's noontime or to refuse to eat your noon meal? If watches are a few seconds or even a few minutes different from each other, they can still be basically telling you the right time, and you'd be crazy to refuse food at mealtime until all timepieces were perfectly synchronized with each other. Likewise, many good churches may not agree exactly on all points, but if they are sound on basic truths, you will benefit from whatever Bible-based, Christ-honoring church you join, and you'd be foolish to say you were going to wait for all the churches to be perfectly the same. As you put on the belt of truth, be sure to join the community of truth, the forces of truth united under the leadership of Jesus.

Let me ask again: have you buckled on the belt of truth? Do you buckle it on again each new day? Start every day by reading part of God's Word personally. If you have a spouse and children, focus on God's truth together as a family. Then band together with a church. Encourage each other in the truth, and join forces in spreading the truth to others. Don't go anywhere without the belt of truth. You can't fight Satan effectively if you're uncertain or confused or just plain wrong. Study the truth. Ask God to increase how much you know and to help you believe more clearly and more firmly than ever. "Stand firm then, with the belt of truth buckled around your waist."

Chapter Eleven

The Breastplate of Righteousness

...with the breastplate of righteousness in place... (Ephesians 6:14)

If you were fighting a battle, what would you want to wear? With artillery firing and shrapnel flying, would you rather be wearing a baseball cap or a heavy-duty helmet? If an enemy was using poison gas against you, would you rather be wearing designer sunglasses or a gas mask? If a sniper was aiming bullets at your heart, would you rather be wearing a light T-shirt or body armor? If you were advancing against an enemy position, would you rather be riding in a golf cart or an armor-plated tank? If you were in a war, you would want the best protection you could get.

Protective equipment isn't always colorful or comfortable. A combat helmet is not nearly as soft and pleasant as a baseball cap. A gas mask is more awkward and ugly than designer sunglasses. Body armor is heavier and hotter than a T-shirt. A tank is noisier than a golf cart, and a tank doesn't catch cool breezes or give a nice view like a golf cart does. But in battle, none of that matters. You care more about solid protection than about style or short-term comfort. You care more about staying alive for the long term than about how you feel or look for the moment.

That's common sense for any soldier in a battle, and it also makes sense for the ultimate conflict against Satan. You need strong protection, whether it seems pleasant to you or not. It's more important to live forever and to avoid the horror of hell than to do whatever seems easiest at the moment. To survive the attacks of Satan and have eternal life, you need the armor of God, even if you think other clothing would be more comfortable.

Among the various pieces in the armor of God is "the breastplate of righteousness." At the time the Bible was written, soldiers used different gear than modern troops, but the basic principle of protection was the same. Every piece of armor was important, and the breastplate was second to none. The breastplate extended from the base of the neck down to the abdomen. It covered the torso, the trunk of the body. The breastplate protected the heart, lungs, liver, and other vital organs. The breastplate was less comfortable than an ordinary shirt or tunic, but it provided far better protection against swords, spears, and arrows. In the armor God provides for spiritual warfare, righteousness is the breastplate that protects the heart, the very core of our being, the wellspring of life.

Righteousness may not sound very appealing. The very word can almost cause an allergic reaction. For some of us, "righteousness" sounds like an impossible standard, something to make us feel like rotten failures. For others, the word "righteousness" is associated with being a stiff, pompous, holier-than-thou perfectionist. Just the mention of righteousness makes us feel awkward and uncomfortable. But don't let that discomfort turn you off to righteousness before you find out what it really is and how much you need it. Righteousness may sound unpleasant, but so does the roar of a heavily armored tank. Righteousness may seem hard and unstylish, but so is a combat helmet. Righteousness may appear ugly to you, but a gas mask isn't exactly pretty. Righteousness may feel too heavy, but a breastplate or a bulletproof vest is heavier than a flimsy T-shirt. So if talk of righteousness makes you feel awkward or uncomfortable, hang in there. The goal is to be alive for the long term—for eternity—not just to go with whatever you happen to like at the moment. You should want righteousness no matter how little it appeals to you, simply because you can't survive without it.

Let me add, however, that if you really examine this breastplate and put it on, you'll discover that it's not so unpleasant after all. Righteousness is not so hard, heavy, and clunky as you'd think a piece of armor would be. The breastplate of righteousness is very strong and resistant to evil attacks—stronger than the equipment of any army— but it also turns out to be beautiful, comfortable, enjoyable, and precious beyond price.

Alien Righteousness

What is righteousness? It is meeting God's standard and being right with him. Righteousness is measuring up to God's perfect character and being able to relate to him and have access to him. Without righteousness, you have no relationship with God, and you perish in hell without him.

Where can you get this righteousness? Many religions of the world see the importance of having some sort of righteousness. They see that morality matters. To that de- gree these religions are correct. Where they go wrong is that they offer do-it-yourself righteousness. They tell you how to earn your own righteousness and how to make yourself measure up to the level God requires. This is a fatal error. You can try your hardest to do good things, but you can't measure up to God's righteousness. You can put yourself through painful sacrifices to make up for sins, but such penance can't atone for the wrongs you've done. You can try every pilgrimage, every ritual, every relic, every method of meditation, but such things can never give you access to God's throne room.

If you follow a religion that tells you how to earn your own righteousness, you get tangled in at least two lies. First, you lie to yourself about God's standard and imagine God's righteousness to be lower than it really is. Second, you lie to yourself about your character and conduct, and you imagine yourself to be higher than you really are. Every religion that teaches righteousness by your own effort drives you to think of God at too low a level and yourself at too high a level. How else could you bring yourself to God's level of righteousness? You can't afford to see how high God truly is or how low sin really is. Otherwise, you would have to admit that God's righteousness is impossible for you.

Righteousness is absolutely necessary, yet utterly impossible for any of us to achieve. Man-made religion can teach man-made righteousness, but this can't save anybody. Righteousness means measuring up to God's standard, and that is something you and I cannot do. We cannot build our own breastplate of righteousness, so where can we get it? The answer is that we must have alien righteousness.

The word *alien* may bring to mind odd critters from other galaxies flying around in spaceships. But alien righteousness has nothing to do with UFOs or science fiction. *Alien* means "other, someone else, someone very different." To have alien righteousness means that I somehow get the righteousness of someone else, someone very different from myself. It means that someone alien to me, someone who is not sinful like me, someone who measures up to God's standard and is at God's level, somehow transfers his righteousness to me. Such righteousness is alien to my fallen, sinful character, but this alien righteousness must somehow count as mine, even though it comes from someone else and not from me. The only righteousness that can make an effective breastplate is God's righteousness in Jesus Christ transferred to me.

Alien righteousness is the complete opposite of self-righteousness. Self-righteousness is not part of the armor of God; it is one of Satan's favorite weapons to destroy us. Trusting your own righteousness is like putting on a breastplate with long, sharp spikes on the side that goes next to your body. The more tightly the breastplate is strapped on, the deeper the spikes press into you. Satan is happy to help you put it on. He needs no other weapon against you if he can strap you so tightly in self-righteousness that it pierces your heart and destroys you.

Satan loves to use religion to destroy people, to make them enemies of God and sometimes even killers of other people. This has happened to far too many religious people. Trusting their own righteousness, they think they measure up to God's standard. If they fall a bit short, they think they can make up for it and rise to God's level by killing God's enemies in holy wars or by giving their lives in battle against the infidels. This has happened at various times in history, and it still haunts our world today. But inflicting pain on others or absorbing pain ourselves cannot atone for sin and make us righteous. Homicidal murderers and suicidal martyrs cannot use blood to escape guilt and raise themselves to God's level. Only the blood of Christ can pay the price, remove the guilt, and open the way to heaven.

The apostle Paul knew from personal experience how deadly self-righteousness could be. Paul had grown up in a religious home, and as a young man he tried his hardest to measure up to God's standard. He was proud of his right-eousness and opposed those he thought were out of tune with God. What was the result? Paul hunted Christians, imprisoned them, and killed them, all in the name of doing God's will.

But then this self-righteous, Christian-hating murderer had a direct encounter with the risen Lord Jesus. No longer was Paul proud of his own righteousness—he wanted to take it off and throw it away like garbage. No longer did Paul think he had earned God's approval—he knew he de-served nothing but God's wrath. Paul saw that his old self-made righteousness had made him "a blasphemer and a persecutor and a violent man," and he called himself the chief of sinners (1 Timothy 1:13,15). Speaking of his religious background, his zeal, and his efforts at righteousness, Paul said, "I consider them rubbish, that I may gain Christ and be found in him, not having a righteousness of my own that comes from the law, but that which is through faith in Jesus Christ—the righteousness that comes from God and is by faith" (Philippians 3:8-9).

It was this very same Paul who wrote about the armor of God and told us to have "the breastplate of righteousness in place." Clearly this breastplate must not be our own righteousness but alien righteousness, righteousness from beyond us, the righteousness of God in Jesus Christ.

Imputed Righteousness

What does it mean to have the breastplate of righteousness in place? We need the complete righteousness of Jesus *imputed* to us, credited to us, counted as ours apart from anything we do, as the basis for our relationship to God. And once we receive imputed righteousness by faith in God's free gift, we also need *imparted* righteousness, Jesus' character shaping our character.

Maybe you're tempted to say, "Stop throwing strange words at me. Imputed! Imparted! Righteousness isn't a favorite topic to begin with, and these words make it even more complicated and unpleasant." But remember what I said earlier. It's easier to slip into a T-shirt than to strap on body armor, but it's not safer if you're heading into battle. So why be careless and unsafe about your soul? Why be willing to study years and years to prepare for a job in some profession, but unwilling to spend a few minutes preparing our minds for matters of eternal importance? Why think military forces need topnotch training in military technology and strategy, but think that in spiritual warfare it's okay to be lazy and mush-minded? In your walk with God and your battle against Satan, you need to grasp the distinction between imputed and imparted right-eousness. This isn't just theory for theologians. It's protection for ordinary people from Satan's attacks.

Imputed righteousness is an accounting method God uses, in which Jesus' perfection gets credited to your account. The Son of God always had a perfect relationship and union with his Father, even before he came to earth and took a human nature. When he became human, Jesus did what no human before or since has ever done: he kept God's law perfectly. Everything Jesus did, everything he said, everything he thought, was perfectly in line with God's law. Jesus honored his heavenly Father with his whole being. He did his Father's will without sinning even once. He obeyed his Father all the way to laying down his life on the cross. Jesus was and is totally righteous.

If this active obedience, this righteousness of Jesus, is imputed to you, it counts as yours. God transfers Jesus' record to you. You might have a shameful record of sin, but if you put your faith in Jesus, God sees you as he sees Jesus: not guilty, fully accepted in love. But what about your own record of sin and disobedience? That gets put on Jesus' account and is paid fully by the blood he poured out when he died on the cross. Your sin is counted as his, and his righteousness is counted as yours. When you put your faith in Christ, God not only takes away your sins but he also credits to you the perfect obedience of Christ. You don't just get rid of guilt; you get the same right standing as Jesus.

How does imputed righteousness serve as a breastplate against Satan's attacks? It protects from two of Satan's chief weapons: pride and despair. Sometimes Satan tempts you to be proud, to think you've worked your way to God's level of righteousness and to despise others. But if you trust entirely in Jesus' righteousness and regard your own righteousness as rags and rubbish, you are protected from pride. How can you be proud of yourself when your entire standing depends on someone else, on Jesus? The breastplate of imputed righteousness protects from pride.

If Satan can't pierce your heart with pride, he may switch weapons and attack you with doubt and despair. When you do something wrong or when you remember a sin from the past, Satan says, "Do you really think God would accept someone who did something like that? God is holy, and you are bad. God is pure, and you are rotten. Look at the sort of person you are! Look at the things you've done! You might as well forget about eternal life." But with the breastplate of righteousness in place, you tell Satan, "I know everything you're saying. I am sinful, and God is holy. But I look to Jesus, not myself. I don't count on my own ability to measure up. I count on Christ, and God imputes to me Jesus' perfect righteousness. Satan, before you can pierce me with despair, you will have to find something unrighteous in Jesus, for his righteousness is my breastplate." Satan can't handle that. Satan can shoot all sorts of holes in *your* righteousness, but he can't find even one tiny weakness in *Jesus'* righteousness.

If you try to resist despair by working up certain feelings or depending on special experiences, your heart will not survive. But your heart is safe if it is protected by the imputed righteousness of Jesus. This is what the Bible calls "being justified by faith." The word *justified* simply means "counted righteous by God," and when you are counted righteous through faith in Jesus—justified by faith—your heart is protected from Satan's attacks.

Imparted Righteousness

Imputed righteousness is the basis for your entire standing with God, apart from anything you do. Once you have a new standing with God, you need to be made into a new person. Once Jesus' righteous standing before God has fully been imputed to you—that is, credited to your account—his righteous character is then gradually *impart-*

ed to you, that is poured into you, made a part of your being, so that you start thinking, talking, and acting more like Jesus would.

This doesn't happen all at once. *Imparted* righteousness doesn't come in a moment; it comes in ever-growing measure over the course of a lifetime. Unlike imputed righteousness, which is complete the moment God credits Jesus' finished work to you, imparted righteousness is not complete until God has made your actual character and conduct exactly like Jesus. Imputed righteousness is the complete work of Christ credited to you once for all when you put your faith in Jesus. Imparted righteousness is your developing, partial resemblance to Jesus, which is never complete in this life. Only when you go to heaven will you be sinless and perfect like Jesus.

Imparted righteousness is never the basis for your acceptance by God. Rather, the reverse is true: your acceptance by God is the basis for imparted righteousness. The complete righteousness of Jesus must be credited to you before you can be accepted by God and start to develop into a person like Jesus. God accepts you only on the basis of complete, perfect, imputed righteousness that is not your own, and once he accepts you, his Holy Spirit begins the process of making you more and more like Jesus. This ongoing process of imparting more and more righteousness to your actual character and conduct is what the Bible calls "being sanctified" or "made holy."

To ward off Satan's attacks on your heart, you must know the difference between imputed righteousness and imparted righteousness, between justification and sanctification. The moment you start thinking that your acceptance with God depends on your progress in becoming like Christ, you will either be puffed up with pride by overestimating your progress, or you will be cast down in despair at how little progress you've made. To be secure, you absolutely must depend on justification by faith in the finished work of Christ imputed to you. Once you realize that Satan can't destroy your standing with God, you are set free to live in the same kind of joyful, loving obedience that Jesus gave to his heavenly Father.

Imputed righteousness is your chief protection against self-righteousness, pride, and despair, but that doesn't mean imparted righteousness has no place at all in the breastplate of righteousness. Satan can't fatally wound and bring to hell anyone to whom God has credited Jesus' perfection, but Satan can still inflict a lot of wounds that are not fatal to the soul but are still very painful and damaging. The more righteous we become in character, the harder it becomes for Satan to tempt us successfully and wound our spirits. We need more and more of the Holy Spirit's life and power, more and more of Jesus, more and more healthy patterns and less enslavement to old habits, in order to be vigorous, effective warriors for Christ. Also, imparted righteousness can strengthen our assurance of salvation. If there's not even a hint of imparted righteousness growing in us, we might be mistaken in thinking that the full righteousness of Christ has already been imputed to us. Those God accepts fully and freely in Christ, he also begins to transform.

Imparted righteousness can serve as a fruit of spiritual life which encourages confidence that God has accepted us for Jesus' sake, and the more righteousness becomes part of our being, the harder it is for Satan to tempt us successfully and the easier it becomes for us to advance against Satan and attract others to the beauty of the Savior.

Mithril from Christ

Earlier we saw that in a military conflict, we're more concerned about solid protection than about style or short-term comfort, and that we should seek the breastplate of righteousness, even if it might seem uncomfortable and ugly, simply because our survival depends on it. But once you understand righteousness and put it on as a breastplate, once you know the wonder of God justifying you for Jesus' sake and sanctifying you to become more like him, you find that righteousness isn't unpleasant and ugly after all. It's more like the mithril coat of mail worn by the hobbit Frodo in J. R. R. Tolkien's *The Lord of the Rings.*

In Tolkien's tales, Frodo's mithril coat provides powerful protection. More than once, it saves Frodo from being stabbed to death. Still, even though it provides life-saving protection, mithril is light and lovely. Frodo's mithril coat is so precious that it is worth more than the wealth of the entire Shire, the neighborhood where Frodo grew up. Frodo could never have made this mithril coat himself, and he could never have come up with enough wealth to purchase something so precious. Someone else made it. How did Frodo get it? He received it as a gift from someone else.

Mithril isn't just Tolkien's legend; the breastplate of righteousness is mithril. The breastplate of righteousness is not heavy, ugly self-righteousness but the light, lovely righteousness of Jesus Christ. This breastplate is made of the loving obedience of Jesus to his heavenly Father, who prizes his eternal Son more than all the treasure in the universe. This breastplate, given freely to us as a gift, is paid for by the blood of Jesus, of which one drop is more precious than all the splendor of men and angels. We could never make such a mighty protection for ourselves. We could never earn such a precious adornment. But it can be ours simply by accepting God's gift and putting it on. This mithril breastplate of Christ's righteousness is strong enough to turn aside Satan's every attack on our heart, and it is beautiful enough to make angels marvel at our splendor in Christ. Accept God's gift. Stand against Satan with the mithril breastplate of righteousness in place to defend you, and you can also stand before God with that same breastplate to adorn you and make you beautiful enough to belong in heaven.

Chapter Twelve

A Soldier's Footwear

...with your feet fitted with the readiness that comes from the gospel of peace. (Ephesians 6:15)

Achilles had a teeny, tiny problem with his foot. The hero of Greek myth had a body that could not be injured, except for a little spot on his heel. Back when Achilles was a baby, his mother, Thetis, tried to make him immortal by dipping him in the river Styx. The magical water gave total protection to anything it touched. But Thetis held her baby by his heel, and that part of Achilles' foot was not touched by the protective water.

Achilles grew up to be the mightiest warrior among the Greeks. He joined the Greek forces in the campaign against the kingdom of Troy and defeated every enemy he faced. He conquered various villages and killed Troy's fiercest warriors, including the mighty prince Hector. No weapon could hurt Achilles. No warrior could beat Achilles. But then Prince Paris of Troy shot a poisoned arrow that happened to strike Achilles at his only weak point, that teeny, tiny spot on his foot. The poison did its deadly work, and that was the end of Achilles. He died.

Shaquille O'Neal had a teeny, tiny problem with his foot. Such a small problem on such a big man wouldn't seem to matter. In 2002, the giant basketball star had just led the Los Angeles Lakers to a third straight championship, and looking ahead to the new season, a fourth championship seemed almost certain. But the Lakers began the season as losers, with Shaq on the sidelines. He had only one small problem: a bad toe. The toe had required surgery, and Shaq sat out the first twelve games of the new season. Shaq still stood over seven feet tall and weighed over 320 muscular pounds, but that didn't help as long as his toe needed to recover. No opposing player could stop Shaq, but the toe stopped him. The world champions suddenly looked as bad as any team in the league. Playing without Shaq, they lost nine of their first twelve games. Even after he returned to the court, the Lakers lost 19 of their first thirty games. Eventually the toe recovered, and Shaquille O'Neal and the Lakers again became a force to reckon with. The difference between being champions and losers was one toe.

Small weaknesses can cause huge problems. That's true not just in Greek myths or professional basketball but in spiritual warfare as well. Satan is always looking for a weakness to exploit. He looks for ways to turn small sins into big problems that destroy people forever. Something starts as a small doctrinal error, and Satan finds a way to turn it into a huge heresy. Something starts as a careless choice, and Satan finds a way to make it a deadly addiction. Something starts as a little quarrel between husband and wife, and Satan turns it into a grudge and a divorce. Something starts as a minor disagreement between nations, and Satan turns it into a war. Something starts as a little step away from God, and Satan turns it into the highway to hell. Satan is an expert in this. He looks you over, searching for a weak spot. It might seem small and unimportant, but Satan can use it to bring you down.

With an enemy like that, partial protection isn't enough. You need total protection. When the Bible talks about spiritual warfare and the armor of God, it doesn't just say to put on a few parts of the armor to protect what you think is most important. It says to put on the *full* armor of God. It says to use every piece of equipment, covering even parts of the body that might seem less important—such as the feet. Ephesians 6:15 says to have "your feet fitted with the readiness that comes from the gospel of peace."

Proper Footwear

For a soldier in biblical times, it was dangerous to have unprotected feet. The main danger was not a poisoned arrow in the heel, as in the legend of Achilles—that didn't happen very often. But there were other dangers for a soldier with unprotected feet. If you were in a fight and you slipped and fell because of bad shoes, your opponent might kill you before you could regain your feet. If you were marching barefoot over an area with thorns and sharp stones, your feet might be so torn up that you wouldn't even make it to the battle front. If you charged an enemy position that was fortified with short, sharp stakes in the ground, unprotected feet would be pierced, you would fall to the ground in pain, and your enemy could easily finish you off. If you marched in an area that had scorpions or poisonous snakes and didn't have proper protection, a bite or a sting could lay you low. If you had to march in mud or cold weather without proper footwear, cold and wetness could make you sick. Fevers and other illnesses destroyed many soldiers.

Strong armies understood the importance of a soldier's feet. The bottom of their footwear had thick soles, enabling them to walk in dangerous areas without injury. Often this footwear also had spikes on the bottom to provide firm footing, prevent slipping, and help the soldier hold his ground. What a soldier wore on his feet might seem less important than how he protected his head and chest, but wise generals and soldiers knew that a foot problem could be as bad as any problem. It could lead to death, and even if a soldier didn't die, injured feet or illness could make him totally useless for combat, more of a hindrance than a help to the cause he was serving. A soldier's feet needed proper protection to help him survive and to give him mobility to go wherever his commander told him.

When the Bible talks about spiritual warfare against sin and Satan, it urges us to put on the full armor of God, including the right footwear. There may be areas of life that don't seem very important, but if we're careless in little things, Satan can use them to destroy us or to make us ineffective in the service of Christ. To stay on your feet amid Satan's attacks, to hold your ground against the devil, to march wherever Christ calls, and to triumph in the Lord, you need proper footwear. You need "your feet fitted with the readiness that comes from the gospel of peace."

A soldier needs proper footwear not just for defensive reasons but also to go on the offensive. The goal in warfare is not just holding ground but marching forward, not just survival but victory. Some of the great military campaigns of history depended on the ability of armies to move faster and farther than their enemies thought possible—and the ability to march was helped by equipping soldiers with excellent footwear. The armies of Alexander the Great and Julius Caesar had brilliant leadership and excellent weapons; they also took good care of their feet. This enabled them to move swiftly and surely, to outmaneuver opponents, and to win amazing victories.

Likewise, in spiritual warfare, the goal is not just survival but victory. The aim is not just to avoid defeat but to drive back the evil one and take territory away from him. To put it another way, the aim is not just to resist Satan and avoid hell personally but also to spread the message of eternal life to others, win them to faith in Jesus, and bring more parts of life under Jesus' life-giving rule. "The readiness that comes from the gospel of peace" is vital for defense and for offense: it enables you to stand firm and defend yourself when Satan attacks, and it enables you to go on the offensive and march forward to victory under Jesus' direction.

When Ephesians 6:15 says to have "your feet fitted with the readiness that comes from the gospel of peace," what does it mean? For a soldier of Christ, readiness means that you are ready to stand firm and fight off Satan, and it means you are ready to move into enemy-occupied territory, win victories for Jesus, and carry out the mission he gives you. Where does such readiness come from? The gospel of peace. The word *gospel* means "good news" or "glad tidings." In Isaiah 52:7, the Bible says, "How beautiful ... are the feet of those who bring good news, who proclaim peace, who bring good tidings, who proclaim salvation, who say..., 'Your God reigns!'" The gospel is good news because it is the glad message of peace: peace with God, peace in your heart, peace spread to others.

Peace With God

In spiritual warfare, a soldier of Christ must wear combat boots of peace. Isn't that a contradiction? How can war bring peace? How can the footwear of peace serve as combat boots? Well, sometimes the best way to enjoy lasting peace is to first win a war that gets rid of a constant threat to peace. And sometimes the best way to win a war against a strong enemy is to make peace with a different enemy who is even stronger and who then becomes your ally in the war you need to win.

Suppose you're a weak nation being attacked by a cruel, aggressive nation that won't leave its neighbors alone. The only way to have peace is war. The only hope of peace is to defeat that nation and be free from its aggression. But what if you're not strong enough to win this war? Well, suppose there's a third nation that is strongest of all. It's a good, peaceful, free nation, and it has the power to defend you and defeat your attacker. If that nation were your ally, you'd win for sure.

There's just one problem: you're not at peace with the good nation. That nation has never wronged you, but you still resent that nation; you've gone against its interests many times, and you've done various things to make yourself its enemy. This nation doesn't wish you ill. It isn't eager to destroy you, and it certainly isn't on the side of your evil enemy, but why should it help you if you remain at odds with it? If it wanted to punish you, it wouldn't even need to attack you directly. It could simply leave you to the cruelty of your vicious enemy. To win a war against the nasty enemy, your only hope is to get on peaceful, friendly terms with your good enemy. Peace with the good enemy is the key to winning the war with the evil enemy.

Satan is an aggressive enemy. War against Satan is the only means to lasting peace, and making peace with God is the key to winning the war against Satan. Satan is stronger than we are, but God is stronger than Satan. The Lord will defeat Satan for us, but only if we're at peace with God.

But how can you have a peace treaty with God if you're his enemy? People who sin and go against God's will—that's all of us—are by nature "God's enemies" (Romans 5:10). Once we've made ourselves God's enemies, we're doomed, unless God deals with our offenses, forgives our sins, and makes us his friends again.

This is exactly what God has done through the suffering and death of Jesus Christ. Jesus paid the price for our offenses, "making peace through his blood, shed on the cross. Once you were alienated from God and were enemies in your minds because of your evil behavior. But now he has reconciled you [made you his friends] by Christ's physical body through death" (Colossians 1:21-22).

Even after we've gone against God and done all sorts of damage, the Lord chooses to pay for the damage himself instead of requiring us to pay. He chooses to offer us a peace treaty instead of wiping us out or letting Satan wipe us out. This peace treaty, this new covenant, is how we can stop being God's enemies and be his friends instead. In this friendship, this alliance, we no longer face Satan on our own. When we have peace with God, the Lord fights on our behalf. Peace with God is the key to winning the war against Satan, and once that war is won, we will have eternal peace and joy with no more grief or pain.

Do you have peace with God? Have you accepted his peace treaty through faith in Jesus' blood? Peace with God and an alliance with him is entirely the work of Jesus. Accept his treaty by trusting Jesus. It is a horrible offense against the Lord to despise and reject his peace treaty after he has paid for it with his own blood. If you reject Jesus, you have no protection from Satan, and no defense against God's anger. So trust God's treaty. Accept by faith what Jesus has done, and God will be your ally and defender. Scripture says, "Therefore, being justified by faith, we have peace with God through our Lord Jesus Christ" (Romans 5:1). God is no longer an enemy but our best friend. "If God is for us, who can be against us?" (Romans 8:31). Even Satan himself can't stand against us.

The good news of peace with God equips our feet with readiness. This readiness is like wearing footwear with spikes. Dig in and stand firm against Satan. Don't slip and slide around. Be sure of the gospel. Don't change your mind; keep believing in Jesus. Don't change your mood; keep rejoicing in peace with God. The sturdy footwear of readiness enables you to dig in your spikes and stand firm.

This footwear also enables you to march against Satan in all types of territory. Go on the attack against the evil one. Rescue others from his clutches. Enlist them in God's army. Scripture says, "Always be prepared to give an answer to everyone who asks you to give the reason for the hope that you have" (1 Peter 3:15). Always prepared! Always ready! Have your feet fitted with readiness to share the gospel of peace with others. Tell how they can escape

Satan's attacks and defeat him by accepting peace with
God through faith in Jesus.

Inner Peace

Peace with God is an objective reality based on the
work of Christ and the new covenant treaty established by
God. This objective reality also produces the subjective
experience of inner peace. When you know God is your
friend, you have peace inside that is beyond anything
words can explain. The Bible says, "The peace of God,
which transcends all understanding, will guard your hearts
and your minds in Christ Jesus" (Philippians 4:7).

The inner *feeling* of peace depends on the outer *reality*
of peace with God. Some people try to make you feel better without actually making anything better. They like to
say, "Peace" when there is no peace (Ezekiel 13:10). Nothing can really set your heart at peace except to know that
you are right with God. William Gurnall's classic *The
Christian in Complete Armor* says:

> It would not help a condemned man on the road to
> execution if you put a fragrant rose in his hand and
> advised him to smell the flower and feel better
> about everything. He would still see the gallows
> just ahead. If a messenger from the prince should
> press a pardon into his hand, though, he would be
> overcome with joy. But this is the only thing that
> could change the man's heart. Anything short of
> pardoning mercy is as insignificant to a troubled
> conscience as that flower would be in a dying
> man's hands.

Peace with God is the key to inner peace. If you're not
right with God, if you're his enemy, you can't be truly
calm. "The Lord will give you an anxious mind, eyes weary with longing, and a despairing heart. You will live in
constant suspense, filled with dread both night and day,
never sure of your life" (Deuteronomy 28:65-66). Inner

turmoil is often a symptom of being at odds with God. "'There is no peace,' says the Lord, 'for the wicked'" (Isaiah 48:22).

Peace with God is crucial to inner peace. If you're torn up inside by guilty feelings, God's pardon can bring peace. If you're full of anxiety and despair about the future, God's strength can give you peace. Lack of peace with God can sometimes move you to do things that are self-destructive or harmful to others. Something inside us tells us that if something is wrong, somebody's got to pay for it—so we either put ourselves through needless suffering or make other people suffer by being cruel to them. But if we know that Jesus has suffered for us and paid the price to give us peace with God, we have inner peace. This inner peace replaces guilt with assurance, anger with compassion, fear with courage, despair with confidence.

When God makes a peace treaty with you and you feel his peace in your heart, you become a fearless warrior for God. Satan loses his ability to intimidate you. Satan will attack your heart, but if your feet are fitted with the readiness that comes from the gospel of peace, your inner peace will stay strong. Thorns and sharp stakes and cruel snakes cannot pierce feet that are protected by peace. Jesus says, "I have given you authority to trample on snakes and scorpions and to overcome all the power of the enemy; nothing will harm you" (Luke 10:19).

Spreading Peace

As we receive peace with God and experience inner peace, we must spread this peace to others. Wear those combat boots of peace! Stand strong against Satan, march forward against him, and bring to other people the good news of God's peace treaty.

In spreading peace, begin at home. Make sure you are at peace with God and that your heart is ruled by peace, not by restlessness and combativeness. Make sure you are at peace with family members and fellow Christians. You can harm yourself and others if you go on the march in campaigns for various causes without the footwear of peace. Your only result may be to upset others and to get upset yourself. When you're truly at peace, you might still upset people, but not as often, and only for the right reasons. The Bible says, "Make every effort to live in peace with all men" (Hebrews 12:14). "If it is possible, as much as it depends on you, live at peace with everyone" (Romans 12:18). Jesus says, "Blessed are the peacemakers, for they will be called sons of God" (Matthew 5:9).

In a war, it's especially important that you be at peace with others who are on your side. Fight the enemy; don't fight each other. If members of a military unit are lobbing grenades at each other and shooting at their fellow troops, how can they ever defeat the enemy? They are defeating themselves. The Bible tells church people who bring lawsuits against each other, "The very fact that you have lawsuits among you means you have been completely defeated already" (1 Corinthians 6:7). William Gurnall says that church people bickering with each other are like navy shipmates arguing with each other while an enemy is drilling a hole in the bottom of their ship. Satan loves to stir up disputes among Christians.

Arguments with fellow believers might not always seem so serious—a little gossip here, a little grudge there, a little dispute over music now and then. But remember Achilles' heel and Shaquille O'Neal's toe. A teeny, tiny foot problem can turn a champion athlete into a loser and a military hero into a dead man. A teeny lack of peace in the conscience, a tiny lack of peace with fellow Christians, can make our feet vulnerable to injury and disable our effectiveness against Satan. God's people must be at peace within their own hearts and at peace with each other in order to stand up to Satan's attacks and march against him.

Christians, let's unite with each other and proclaim God's gospel of peace to the world. Are your feet fitted with readiness to take back territory from Satan and win people for Christ? Don't be slowed by those who say you shouldn't call people of other cultures and other countries to Christ. Jesus says, "Go and make disciples of *all* nations" (Matthew 28:19). Don't be held back by those who say all religions are equally helpful and who say you should leave everyone to their own religion and not try to lead them to faith in Jesus. Jesus does not say every religion works equally well. Jesus says, "No one comes to the Father except through me" (John 14:6). Not everyone agrees with that, but that's what Jesus says, and I'm not about to contradict the Son of God.

Religion doesn't give peace with God; only Jesus does. Religion doesn't give lasting inner peace; only Jesus does. Religion doesn't have power to defeat Satan; only Jesus does. Religion doesn't give eternal life; only Jesus does. Religion doesn't have the power to bring world peace; only Jesus does. World peace will occur only after Satan has been defeated, his lies have been debunked, and Jesus comes again to bring the whole world under his reign of peace. True peace comes only through the gospel of peace.

Believe that gospel, and then go on the march to spread it everywhere. Jesus is on a mission, and he calls you to join his mission. The Bible says, "He himself is our peace... He came and preached peace to you who were far away and peace to those who were near" (Ephesians 2:14,17). To all whose feet are fitted with the readiness of the gospel of peace, the Bible promises: "The God of peace will soon crush Satan under your feet" (Romans 16:20). "Now may the Lord of peace himself give you peace at all times and in every way" (2 Thessalonians 3:16).

Chapter Thirteen

Shielded from Arrows

Take up the shield of faith, with which you can extinguish all the flaming arrows of the evil one. (Eph. 6:16)

Saturday night tends to be my hardest night of the week. If something goes wrong, it doesn't happen just any night. It usually happens Saturday night. If our computer crashes, it happens on Saturday evening. If our fire alarm system gets messed up and goes off, it happens Saturday night, waking the whole family and ruining our sleep. If our children are sick, Saturday night seems to be the favorite time for illness, keeping children and parents awake most of the night. If there's a ferocious storm and we lose electricity, it happens Saturday night. If there's a torrential downpour and our basement is in danger of flooding, it happens Saturday night, and I'm awake much of the night hoping to prevent trouble.

Why does Saturday night seem to be my worst night of the week? I don't think it's a coincidence. I think it happens because I'm a preacher of the gospel, and Satan wants to weaken me. On Sunday mornings I must speak to people who need God's Word. That's harder to do if I'm short on sleep and have too many hassles on my mind. Sometimes I've had to preach on less than two hours of sleep the night before because of all the things that went wrong. Satan likes to fire volleys to weaken me and keep me from bringing God's Word in its full, saving power.

Saturday nights are often hard, and so are Sunday mornings. It's harder than usual for our family to get along on Sunday mornings, and that's true of other churchgoing people as well. Friends tell me that their children seem to be at their worst on Sunday morning. The kids argue and pick on each other more than usual. At Sunday breakfast they spill more than usual. The parents are more short-tempered than usual. Family members sometimes yell at each other eating breakfast, getting dressed, and even in the car on the way to church. When they get to church, they might feel so upset or so guilty that they feel they shouldn't even be there.

Are those miserable Sunday mornings a coincidence? I don't think so. Sunday worship is vital for Christians, so Satan fires volley after volley after volley, trying to break us down and prevent us from getting built up and strengthened in church. I know that some problems arise from ordinary weariness and grumpiness, and I'm not the sort of person who blames every little problem on a demon. But I take the Bible seriously when it says that our struggle is not just against flesh and blood but against the spiritual forces of evil. I believe Scripture when it talks about "the flaming arrows of the evil one."

Flaming Arrows

Satan picks certain times to fire his volleys of arrows. He picks Saturday nights and Sunday mornings to wound worshipers before they gather in God's name, and that's far from his only time to shoot his volleys. Many of Satan's worst attacks are timed to strike people when they are about to start a new chapter in their life.

If you have ignored God for years but then start to get interested in the Bible and in Jesus, a lot of Satan's arrows are likely to fly your way. He will fire distractions and all sorts of things that make you feel too busy to get serious about God. If someone has been talking to you about the

Lord, you may suddenly find yourself so busy with lots of stuff that you feel you don't have time to talk with your Christian friend. If you start visiting a church, Satan will try to fill your Sunday mornings with other things to do, or he will help you to focus on things you don't like about the church's music or its members or even its paint or its carpet or a pothole in the parking lot. Even better, in Satan's view, is a rude remark from a church member or a blunder by the pastor—anything that gets your focus away from Jesus and your need for him. The Bible says that the best defense against Satan's flaming arrows is the shield of faith, and if Satan thinks you're getting close to faith, he wants to strike before you get that shield.

But Satan's not the only one at work. God is also active, and he can give you faith despite all Satan's attacks. When that happens, Satan may try to destroy you before you learn to use your shield well. New Christians often face worse troubles and stronger temptations than ever before. Even if there's a healthy, positive change in you, your friends and family may not like it. When you became a Christian, you may have expected your family life to improve, but sometimes it gets worse. You lose some friends, and there's more conflict than ever with family members. If that happens, the problem may be more than just humans not getting along. It may be Satan's fiery arrows. You may also have a harder time with your job and finances. A voice in your minds says, "Christianity is supposed to make life better, but it's getting worse. Life was better before I became a Christian." That little voice isn't just your own thought; it's Satan's suggestion. "You'll be happier if you just forget this religion stuff and go back to the way things were."

Satan times his attacks for greatest effect. A student from a Christian family leaving home for the first time and going to a university is a prime target for arrows of doubt and temptation. You meet smart people who sneer at the

Bible, and something in your mind says over and over, "Is the Bible really true? Does God really exist? Is Jesus really the only Savior? How do you know? The people at this university are a lot smarter than the people in your family and church. What did those folks back home really know?" The voice that whispers these doubts is not just your own mind at work; it is the voice of Satan.

When you go to the university, you might not come across any new fact or strong reasoning against the Bible, and yet you somehow feel that it's not intellectually respectable to trust Scripture and take God at his word. If you really knew the truth about your unbelieving professors and fellow students, you might find that their wisdom isn't so great, that their minds are muddled and their lives are a mess, but Satan doesn't show you the mess. He makes unbelief seem smart and sophisticated.

As Satan fires darts of doubt at your mind, he also fires arrows of temptation at your will and conscience. Satan can fire his arrows of temptation at any time, but he often fires his strongest volleys at those who are entering a new phase of life, such as leaving home for college or the military. He makes drunkenness, drugs, and sex appear the height of happiness. Away from home for the first time, you're free at last, free from rules and inhibitions, free to have fun, free to enjoy yourself! Satan's arrows inflame your desires and put a cloud of smoke over your thinking. Diseases, addictions, broken hearts, and hellfire can spring from such behavior, but the smokescreen of Satan may keep you from seeing this.

Satan is clever in his timing. He is firing various darts all the time, but he reserves his major volleys either for times when we are most vulnerable and unprotected or else for times when we are about to get close to God or attempt something important for the Lord. When you're about to open your Bible, a thousand different thoughts fly into your mind. Even if you're usually very good at focusing your mind, even if you're usually able to think through a complex business project or to concentrate on a difficult scientific theory, you suddenly find it hard to focus when you open a Bible. You may be able to carry on long conversations with people, but when you try to pray and have a conversation with God, your mind suddenly goes blank or is interrupted by all sorts of things. This gets discouraging. You may wonder, "Why is it so hard for me to read the Bible? Why is my mind on so many other things? Why are my prayers interrupted by all these distracting thoughts?" You might think it's just lack of concentration, but it may be a round of missiles from Satan. The sooner you know you're under attack, the sooner you can deal with it.

Another occasion when Satan is most likely to attack is when you are about to do something for God that threatens him. Missionaries are often targets of fierce persecution or of dreadful attacks of discouragement. A church experiencing spiritual revival often comes under demonic attack. In nations that were mostly non-Christian, any growth in the number of Christians is often met by ferocious resistance. Satan is quick to attack anyone who begins a new work for God.

Perhaps the hardest year of my life was my very first year as a pastor. My wife was in the hospital for seven weeks. Our child was in the hospital almost six months and then died. I struggled against doubt, against a sense of being overwhelmed. I think Satan wanted to crush my spirit before I could get started preaching the gospel. God is stronger than Satan, of course, and the Lord carried my wife and me through that awful time. I'm still preaching the gospel today. But Satan and his demons didn't make it easy.

If you work to win people to Jesus, Satan will attack you. The more effective you are, the more arrows he will fire at you. Satan isn't stupid—he doesn't ignore those who are a threat to his cause. If you are spreading the gospel, helping other people, and working to make your community and your country better, don't expect Satan to stand idly by. He will try to wipe you out, and if he can't destroy you, he will try to cripple you and limit your effectiveness.

Satan gets especially upset when his own tactics are exposed and God's armor is presented for people's protection. When C.S. Lewis wrote about the methods of demons in *The Screwtape Letters*, he said, "It almost smothered me before I was done." As for myself, writing about spiritual warfare has been hard. I have often felt burdened or distracted or severely tempted. When I get close to the front lines of battle, Satan comes after me. If you get close to the front lines, he will come after you. If you get serious about fighting sin and leading others to God, you might as well expect a lot of flaming arrows to fly your way.

A Strong Shield

We must be alert to Satan's fiery arrows, and we must have a missile shield to protect us, a shield that makes the arrows bounce off, a shield that even puts out their fire. What shield can do this? The shield of faith. In Ephesians 6, the Bible talks about "the evil day" when Satan's attacks are especially fierce, and urges us to put on God's armor. "In addition to all this," says Ephesians 6:16, "take up the shield of faith, with which you can extinguish all the flaming arrows of the evil one."

At the time these words were written, the shield was a vital part of a soldier's equipment. The shield was usually quite large: about four feet high and about two and a half feet wide. If you held the shield in front of you during hand-to-hand combat, it provided much protection, and the shield was even more important when someone was firing at you from a distance.

Modern military forces often launch air attacks before ground attacks. Missiles and bombs prepare the way and destroy much of the opposing force before ground forces move in. The technology was different in earlier times, but the principle was much the same: shoot from a distance before closing in for hand-to-hand combat. Generals would order archers to shoot volleys of arrows at the enemy from a distance. If the arrows did enough damage, the attackers would close in and finish off their opponents. Attacking archers fired sharp arrows that could pierce the body, and some fired flaming arrows. They would put something flammable on the arrow, set it on fire, and shoot it at the enemy. If you faced a barrage of these flaming arrows and didn't want to be pierced or burned, you needed a shield that was too strong for arrows to go through, and you needed a shield that was fireproof.

When Satan fires his flaming arrows, you need a strong shield, a shield that can't be penetrated, that can't be burned, that can even put out fires. Faith is the shield that can do this. God promises that the shield of faith "can extinguish all the flaming arrows of the evil one." God doesn't say faith *might* be able to do this; he says it *can*. It's not just a possibility; it's a certainty. Faith doesn't just *repel* Satan's arrows and make them bounce off; it puts them out, it *extinguishes* their hellish fire. Faith can put out not just *some* of Satan's arrows but *all* of them, every last one. Faith protects not just from little problems but from the very worst attacks. Faith has power to deal not only with human opposition or the attacks of lesser demons but also from the fiercest attacks of *the evil one*, Satan himself. Not the deadliest arrow in Satan's arsenal, not the fiercest volley he can fire, is too much for faith to deal with. The shield can handle the worst attacks from the prince of darkness himself, so it can surely handle any lesser attacks as well.

Why is this shield so strong? Because God is so strong. When faith is your shield, *God* is your shield. God told Abraham, the father of believers, "I am your shield" (Genesis 15:1). Moses told God's people, "Who is like you, a people saved by the Lord? He is your shield" (Deuteronomy 33:29). King David said, "The Lord is my strength and my shield; my heart trusts in him, and I am helped" (Psalm 28:7). The book of Proverbs declares, "Every word of God is flawless; he is a shield to those who take refuge in him" (Proverbs 30:5). There are so many Bible passages that speak of God as a shield that I can't quote them all here, but I trust you get the point. The power of faith comes not from the one who believes but from the one we believe in. The shield of faith is not faith in yourself or faith in positive thinking or faith in faith; the only faith that can shield you from Satan's attacks is faith in God as the ultimate protection. Faith is confidence in God, belief in his truth, assurance of his promises. Faith is God's means of applying his power and protection to us personally.

Take Up the Shield

When Ephesians 6:16 says to "take up the shield of faith," it calls on us to apply our trust in God to our particular situation and to any attack we are facing. A shield is not merely something to own but something to take up and use. When Jesus' disciples were sometimes defeated by doubt or snared by sin, Jesus would ask them, "Where is your faith?" (Luke 8:25) They were already believers, but sometimes they would forget their faith, almost as though they had mislaid it. Jesus wanted them to find their faith back and make use of it. What about your faith? If you don't have any faith at all, you need to be born again and trust Jesus for eternal life. And even if you do have faith, remember that faith isn't just something to have but something to use. Dr. Martyn Lloyd-Jones, writing about the shield of faith, says, "Faith here means the ability to apply quickly what we believe so as to repel everything the devil does or attempts to do to us."

When Satan fires flaming arrows of *doubt*, take up the shield of faith and put out those arrows. Don't try to defeat doubt by clever reasoning or by gathering evidence. Satan "has sharper reasoning than you," says William Gurnall. "There is more difference between you and Satan than between the weakest idiot and the greatest theologian in the world." Satan is far smarter than you are, and he is a master liar. He is an expert in twisting arguments, evidence, and statistics to support his lies. He can bring up one hard question after another, until your mind spins. Don't try to out-think the devil. Don't try to out-argue him. Don't try to answer every question he brings to your mind. Take up the shield of faith! Extinguish those flaming arrows!

A friend of mine once asked his godly mother, "How do we know the Bible is true?" She responded, "That's from the devil!" That made a deep impact on the young man. From then on he simply believed the Bible without questioning every passage. Questioning isn't always bad. But doubt of God's Word isn't an innocent question; it's a flaming arrow from the devil. If we try to block doubt with a shield of our own thinking skills, we are using a shield of paper against a flaming arrow. Only the shield of faith can stop the arrow of doubt and put out its deadly fire.

If you believe Scripture only when it fits your standards of evidence and reasoning, then you rate human thinking higher than God's Word. The Bible says, "Trust in the Lord with all your heart, and lean not on your own understanding" (Proverbs 3:5). This doesn't mean that God wants you to shut off your brain or that reasoning is bad. Gurnall says,

> Certainly God's gift of reason can confirm His gift of truth. But faith must not depend on reason, but reason on faith. I am not to believe what the Word says merely because it agrees with my reason; but I must believe my reason because it aligns with the Word.

When Satan fires flaming arrows of *temptation*, take up the shield of faith to extinguish those arrows. Don't depend on the shield of your own willpower, or the temptations will overwhelm you. Faith in God's goodness, in his rich blessings and his promise to satisfy your deepest desires, is the best protection against temptation. Faith, not willpower, is your shield.

When arrows of *persecution* come at you, when Satan turns people against you because you belong to Jesus, take up the shield of faith. You may face mockery and job discrimination. In some places you may even face torture and death for Jesus' sake. But take up the shield of faith, and God will be there for you no matter what. Faith says to God, "Your love is better than life" (Psalm 63:3). "Our present sufferings are not worth comparing with the glories that will be revealed in us" (Romans 8:18).

We are hard pressed on every side, but not crushed; perplexed, but not in despair; persecuted, but not abandoned; struck down, but not destroyed... With that same spirit of faith... we know that the one who raised the Lord Jesus from the dead will also raise us with Jesus" (2 Corinthians 4:8-14).

That kind of faith puts out Satan's flaming arrows, so that no amount of persecution can separate you from God or destroy the eternal life that is yours in Christ.

Satan may fire a volley of smaller arrows, *irritations* and problems that may not seem all that dangerous. When I've had a lousy Saturday night before I have to preach Sunday morning, I take up the shield of faith. I don't depend on whether I'm well-rested or in a pleasant mood but on the power of God. Satan may have sapped my energy, but when I'm low on energy, God has as much energy as ever. When I get up to preach his Word, I put my faith in his Holy Spirit to get results, and then the weary state of my own spirit no longer matters. I can brush aside Satan's arrows and extinguish them by the shield of faith.

Some of Satan's worst attacks are his flaming arrows of *accusation*. In fact, the very name Satan means "adversary" or "accuser." He likes to accuse and make you feel guilty for things you haven't actually done. Of course, if you have done wrong, he piles on the guilt and tells you that you're beyond hope.

Have you ever had a horrible thought come into your mind? Satan can send things into your mind so that you have a thought that doesn't really originate with you. You might hate the thought the moment it comes to you and not give in to it at all. But Satan may still try to make you feel guilty about having had such a thought. He may send temptations your way and then make you feel rotten for being tempted, when in fact you should be rejoicing that despite the force of the temptation, God kept you from giving in. It's no sin to be tempted; even Jesus was tempted. If you don't yield, the sin is Satan's, not yours. The tempter is wrong, not the one who resisted temptation.

But what about the times when you do sin? When you know you're guilty, Satan tempts you either to make excuses without repenting, or else he tells you that your sin is too bad for God to forgive. When these arrows of accusation fly at you, take up the shield of faith. You can't earn God's forgiveness, but you don't have to. Forgiveness comes through faith in Jesus' blood. That is your only shield against the accuser. Tell Satan, "My sin is huge, but the value of Jesus' blood is infinitely greater. Satan, if you say my guilt is too great for God, you are lying. Where sin increases, grace increases all the more (Romans 5:20). The Lord rebuke you, Satan. The Lord rebuke you (Zechariah 3:2). You say God can't forgive me, but God says he will. You're a liar, Satan, and God never lies, so I'm going to believe God, not you. God's mercy swallows up my biggest sins as the ocean swallows a rock thrown into it (Micah 7:19). God says that when a search is made for guilt, there won't be any to find, because God's forgiveness will make it vanish completely (Jeremiah 50:20). I am justified by faith, Satan, so away with your accusations."

Friend, beware of Satan's flaming arrows, but be confident in God. When the fiery volleys come, be strong and courageous. "Take up the shield of faith, with which you can extinguish all the flaming arrows of the evil one."

Chapter Fourteen

The Helmet of Salvation

Take the helmet of salvation. (Ephesians 6:17)

The man was terrified. He told me that he was afraid of supernatural spirits. He had grown up in a secular, scientific setting, but he became curious about supernatural powers. He got involved with people who spoke of "white magic." They had a cheerful, appealing view of witchcraft and nature worship. The contact with spirits was exciting, and the nature worship seemed respectful of the environment. At first he enjoyed it, but gradually the spirits grew darker and more evil. Within a few years, he felt trapped by powers he had never dared to imagine. By the time he spoke to me, he desperately wanted to be free, but he had a hard time believing it could happen. How could he escape these terrible powers? How could he recover from the damage to his soul? This man had chosen to get involved with unseen powers, and now he feared he was beyond hope.

Other people don't make a choice to get involved with spirits; they are born into it. If your parents, relatives, and culture are wrapped up in spiritism, you grow up trying to please various spirits—perhaps the spirit of a particular house or river, the spirit of a tree or animal, or the spirit ruling a whole region. You believe your health and success depend on the spirits. If things go well for you, you figure the spirits are favoring you. If something goes wrong, you think a spirit is against you. This can be terrifying. You fear the spirits, and you fear other people who might influence the spirits. If somebody hates you, puts you under a curse, and turns a spirit against you, you might fear that nothing can break the spell. Nothing can save you.

If you grow up with spiritism, it's hard to leave it completely, even if you hear the gospel of Jesus and start calling yourself a Christian. You might be baptized and believe something about Jesus. You might even be taught the truth that Jesus is more powerful than any spirit. But when a crisis hits, you might take the spirits more seriously than you take Jesus. The old traditional religion seems more real than Christianity. If you're having problems, you might not be satisfied to pray to God about them; you might seek help from the old spirits. If you get sick, a tribal healer who knows how to deal with the spirits may seem more valuable to you than a pastor. You may think your illness comes from a spirit that's against you, and the only way to be healed is to perform some ritual or to do something that persuades the spirit to stop afflicting you.

Some people might try to convince you that the spirit world isn't real, that it's all superstition. They might try to make you more scientific and sensible. But that doesn't always help. Some fears and beliefs in spirits are just superstition, but sometimes real demonic powers are involved. Once you've felt the grip of a cruel supernatural power, it doesn't work to deny the supernatural. You know that power is real. The only way you can be free is to have the help of someone with supernatural power even greater than the spirits who are harming you. Only the Lord Jesus Christ is strong enough to save you from all evil spirits.

The Bible speaks of spirits that affect our lives, and the experience of many people confirms that these spirits are real. It won't work to say they're not real. But even if they are real, even if people put curses on you, even if bad spirits attack you, don't be terrified. Don't try to make deals with the spirits. Don't use traditional rituals to appeal to them. Don't try to please the spirits in order to make your life easier. If you do that, you are falling into the spirits' trap. You are playing by their rules, and you'll never win that way. If hostile spirits have hurt you in the past and still want to harm you, don't try to please them. Fight them and defeat them.

Many people are too afraid to fight. They are certain that the spirits control the future, and they don't dare go against them. They don't think they can win. If you feel that way, then your fear will come true—you can't win if you don't expect victory, if you have no hope of salvation, no certainty that your future is in the hands of the Lord Jesus. But if you belong to Jesus and have the sure hope of salvation, you can overcome fear, defeat the demons, and march toward victory. The Bible speaks of wearing "the hope of salvation as a helmet" (1 Thessalonians 5:8).

Satan's Goal

When evil spirits attack, you need a strong helmet. The ruler of the evil spirits is Satan, and he specializes in despair. He knows that if you are hopeless, you are also helpless against him. Satan wants you to think that you don't have a future and that the world doesn't have a future.

To accomplish this goal, Satan and his evil spirits use different tactics with different individuals and different cultures. In some cultures, the spirits make their power obvious in an effort to enslave people. In other cultures, the spirits keep a low profile and seek to undermine belief in anything supernatural, including God. Satan convinces some people and cultures that the spirits of their traditional religion control the future. Satan convinces other people and cultures that the supernatural world doesn't even exist, that there are no spirits and no God, that mechanical laws of nature are the only reality, that there is no life after death for any individual and that the universe itself is headed for a future of total deadness. Satan's methods differ, but his goal is the same: hopelessness.

People who pride themselves on a scientific mindset might not feel bound by enemy spirits, but they can be just as grim about the future. For instance, columnist George Will wrote an article echoing the belief among many educated people that the sun will eventually burn out and all life will be snuffed out. "Earth heads for frigid lifelessness." George Will accepts the theory of biology that our past is rooted in animal ancestors, and he accepts the theory of geology that the earth, which provides humans with a livable environment for the moment, will someday change and make life impossible. "Although the planet is hospitable for the moment, it is indifferent—eventually it will be lethally indifferent—to its human passengers." The secular, scientific mindset is as hopeless as a mindset terrified of hostile spirits. A universe without hope or meaning—this is what Satan wants you to believe.

If you go to schools which teach a mechanical universe, if you think humanity is headed for extinction, you need the hope of salvation as your helmet. The idea that the present world will come to an end and that people are headed for death isn't exactly news, of course. The Bible says the same thing. In Isaiah 51:8 God says, "The heavens will vanish like smoke, the earth will wear out like a garment and its inhabitants die like flies. But my salvation will last forever." Even after you die, even after the world ends, there is new life and a new creation. When you believe that, you have a strong helmet of hope.

The Bible is amazing. It takes the spirit world as seriously as any traditional tribal religion, yet it puts these spirits in their place by declaring the supreme authority of Jesus and his victory over evil spirits. The Bible takes the death of humans and the end of the world as seriously as the grimmest scientific materialist, yet God declares the living hope of resurrection and a new earth. What a difference to have the helmet of salvation! What a difference to know that the ultimate power is not the spirits of traditional religions or the forces of matter and energy but the almighty power of the risen Lord Jesus Christ!

The Blessed Hope

Ephesians 6:17 says, "Take the helmet of salvation." A similar statement in 1 Thessalonians 5:8 speaks of "taking the *hope* of salvation as a helmet." Sometimes when the Bible speaks of salvation, it means having your sins forgiven, being made right with God, and rescued from Satan's grip. In this context, though, the Bible is talking about *final* salvation. The hope of salvation is confidence in the second coming of Jesus, the final defeat of Satan and the forces of evil, the resurrection of the dead, and life in the new heaven and new earth.

This great hope for the future is a strong protection against Satan in the present. To resist Satan's temptations and obey God, you need to be confident that even if evil seems to bring success for the moment, holiness triumphs in the end. This mighty hope enables you to keep saying "No" to Satan and "Yes" to God.

> For the grace of God that brings salvation has appeared to all men. It teaches us to say "No" to ungodliness and worldly passions, and to live self-controlled, upright and godly lives in this present age, while we wait for the blessed hope—the glorious appearing of our great God and Savior, Jesus Christ (Titus 2:11-13).

When the Bible says to take the helmet of salvation, or to take the hope of salvation as a helmet, this is what it means: "we wait for *the blessed hope*—the glorious appearing of our great God and Savior, Jesus Christ."

Don't be trapped by fear of any spirits or spells. Even if such things have dominated you and people around you, Jesus opens up a fantastic future. If you think only about the short term and not the eternal future, you might ask various spirits for help—and it might even work for a time. If you care only about getting over a sickness or improving your income, and if you're willing to sell your soul by seeking help from the spirits, they may help you get what you want, but you will be their slave. Don't let that happen. Trust Jesus. Jesus is more powerful than all the spirits combined, and he can set you free from their grip. Right now he can help you live in spiritual freedom, and at his second coming, he will bring joy to all who trust his salvation.

In the short term, though, Jesus might not give you all the success or health you were hoping for. Does that mean you should give up on Jesus and go back to spirits and try to get favors from them? No, even if Jesus doesn't give you what you want right away, keep trusting him anyway. He knows what's best for you, and if you trust him, you will be glad in the end.

In some traditional religions, the spirits offer ways to get them on your side, or at least to keep them from making you miserable. But these spirits are demons, and it's deadly to deal with demons. Would you make business deals with someone you can't trust, someone who lies constantly? If not, then why try to make deals with Satan? He lies all the time. Sometimes he threatens people who already belong to Jesus and tries to make them think they can't be free from his spirits, but the fact is that a spirit cannot take over the life of someone who belongs to Jesus. If threats don't work for Satan, he and his spirits may promise to make you happier, and they might even give you some short-term results, but their long-term goal is to keep you from Christ and to have you suffer in hell forever. Don't make deals with lying spirits. Even if you get what you want for awhile, don't forget: Satan gladly lets you have less problems if he can bring you to hell forever.

Think of Satan as a general who wants to destroy a country but first needs to get some people on his side before he can wipe them all out. He offers bribes and makes threats to get people on his side, but he still hates those who go along with him. After he has used them, he will torment and ruin them.

Or think of Satan as a murderous crime boss who bullies people to do what he wants or else pays them off to commit criminal acts. Eventually he has them killed after he has no more use for them. People in a crime syndicate may like the extra money and perks their boss gives them, but what good are those favors after he murders them? And even if he lets you live longer, what good are his favors when the crime boss is arrested by the authorities and punished? When he is punished, you also are punished for going along with him and doing his work. Satan is a crime boss who is headed for prison in hell. Those who make deals with him and his spirits will also be imprisoned in hell forever, unless they turn away from Satan to God.

Even so, it can be very tempting to go along with Satan, just as it can be tempting to take bribes to help an enemy general or a crime boss. If they offer you enough money, or threaten harshly enough, you may think your prosperity and your very survival depend on the spirits. But dealing with spirits destroys you in the end. That's why God warns you not to seek help from other spirits or perform rituals to please them. God knows that those spirits only want to use you and ruin you. God wants you to have his joy and eternal life with him. God tells you to pray to him, and only to him. Don't commit treason against God by going along with spirits who are God's enemies.

If these spirits threaten you, don't make deals with them, and don't give in to despair. Take the helmet of salvation! Put your faith in Jesus. Place yourself under his protection right now, and keep looking for Jesus to return. Be ready to meet him. Jesus has already won the decisive battle over Satan, and when he comes again, the victory will be complete. So count on his victory over the evil spirits—don't let the demons fool you. Don't let them bribe and corrupt you with their promises of special favors and powers. Don't let them discourage or crush you with fear. Let the hope of salvation be your helmet.

When you put on the helmet of salvation, you and the Lord have matching helmets. The Bible envisions the Lord putting "the helmet of salvation on his head" and promises, "The Redeemer will come" (Isaiah 59:17,20). When your helmet of salvation matches Jesus' helmet, you are sure to win.

Count On His Coming

How do you put on the helmet of salvation? By counting on Jesus' second coming and looking forward to it. The return of Jesus is not a minor, optional part of Christianity. It is at the heart of the faith, right along with forgiveness through Jesus' death. The Bible says, "Just as man is destined to die once, and after that to face judgment, so Christ was sacrificed once to take away the sins of many people; and he will appear a second time, not to bear sin, but to bring salvation to those who are waiting for him" (Hebrews 9:27-28). If you are born again, you have a future focus. The Bible says God "has given us new birth into a living hope through the resurrection of Jesus Christ from the dead... through faith [you] are shielded by God's power until the coming of the salvation that is ready to be revealed in the last time... you are filled in an inexpressible and glorious joy, for you are receiving the goal of your faith, the salvation of your souls" (1 Peter 1:3-9).

This joyful anticipation of Jesus' coming is a helmet of defense that protects against entanglement with spirits and false religion. It also protects against secularism without a future. Secularism denies the supernatural, teaches that death is the end of us, and that the world will keep running by mechanical laws of nature till it ends in ruin. That hopeless outlook destroys morality and meaning and becomes an excuse to chase pleasure. The Bible says that if this view were true, the logical response would be, "Let us eat and drink, for tomorrow we die" (1 Corinthians 15:32). Have a blast while you last. Why not do anything you please, no matter how wrong it might be, no matter who gets hurt? If there is no God and no eternal future—no rewards for painful sacrifice and no punishment for selfish sin—then pursuing pleasure is the only point of existence. It's no accident that in the pleasure-crazy societies of modern secularism, our educators teach theories which deny the supernatural and deny an eternal future. Satan attacks many minds with such thinking. When your head is under attack, you need a helmet: the hope of salvation.

We saw earlier that people who become Christians after growing up in a culture of spiritism may be tempted to go back to the old spirits when times get tough and Christianity doesn't seem to be getting results. But what if you're a Christian in a culture not of spiritism but of secularism? Well, there too, Satan will try to discourage you in tough times and make you wonder if Christianity is true and worthwhile. He tempts you to give up on the whole thing.

Satan doesn't always try to persuade with clever arguments. Sometimes he tries to overwhelm your faith with disappointment and discouragement. If prayers don't get the answer you want, if year after year goes by without Jesus coming back, you feel disappointed, and Satan makes you wonder if the Lord is real at all. If you've been fighting to be a better person and to make the world a better place but don't see much improvement, you feel discouraged and wonder whether the struggle is worth it. Why keep fighting? If you struggle in your personal life, if you see the church losing ground, if you see society headed in the wrong direction, you may feel like giving up on Christ. You feel worn out, and Satan whispers, "What's the use?

Jesus will never come back. The eternal future is just a dream. The world is the way it has been and always will be. Get real. Give up. Just try to enjoy yourself for a few years before you die."

At such moments, take the helmet of salvation. Remind yourself that God's timing may be different from yours, but that Jesus will surely come to bring salvation to those who are watching for him and working for him. The Bible says,

> Now, brothers, about times and dates we do not need to write you, for you know very well that the day of the Lord will come like a thief in the night... But you, brothers, are not in darkness, so that this day should surprise you. You are all sons of the light and sons of the day... So then, let us not be like others, who are asleep, but let us be alert and self-controlled... putting on faith and love as a breastplate, and *the hope of salvation as a helmet.* For God did not appoint us to suffer wrath but to receive salvation through our Lord Jesus Christ (1 Thessalonians 5:1-9).

When Satan tempts you to give up on Jesus, don't do it. Put on your helmet and say, "God has appointed me to receive salvation. I don't know when the final day will come, but I'm looking forward to it. Meanwhile, I'm not going to let Satan drag me down or discourage me. I'm not going to listen to those who scoff about Jesus' second coming and say it's not going to happen. I'm going to pray that they will come to believe in Jesus and join his cause before it's too late for them. Meanwhile, until Jesus comes, I'm going to take this hope of salvation as my helmet and keep fighting Satan." Keep reminding yourself, "Our salvation is nearer now than when we first believed" (Romans 13:11).

Jesus says there will be hard times before he comes, and some who call themselves Christians will give up.

"Because of the increase of wickedness, the love of most will grow cold," says Jesus, "but he who stands firm to the end will be saved" (Matthew 24:12-13). The helmet of salvation protects you from fear and discouragement so that you can stand firm to the end. You don't have to be terrified by events which terrify other people, especially if these events are signs that we are nearing the end. In fact, when things are at their worst, Jesus may be right at the door. Jesus says, "When these things begin to take place, stand up and lift up your heads, because your redemption is drawing near" (Luke 21:28).

Satan is in the business of despair, of denying a joyful future. Whether he uses secularism or spiritism or some other method, he doesn't want people to see that the future is Jesus. Satan wants non-Christians to keep ignoring the fact that Jesus is coming. Satan wants Christians to get weary of waiting and to give up on Jesus' coming. But Jesus provides the helmet of salvation, the hope of his coming.

If you wear that helmet and live in the hope of Jesus' return, your hope will be rewarded. Jesus promises, "To him who overcomes and does my will to the end, I will give authority over the nations... just as I have received authority from my Father... To him who overcomes, I will give the right to sit with me on my throne, just as I overcame and sat down with my Father on his throne" (Revelation 2:26-27, 3:21). Wear your helmet now, knowing that Jesus will someday replace your helmet with a crown.

Chapter Fifteen

The Sword of the Spirit

Take the sword of the Spirit, which is the Word of God.
(Ephesians 6:17)

In the *Star Wars* movies, what is the ultimate weapon? The light saber. The best warriors are the Jedi knights, and their chief weapon is the light saber. When we turn from the make-believe world of movies to the real world of spiritual warfare, the ultimate weapon is also a light saber. To battle Satan and his demons and the forces of evil, you need something that is both a sword and a light—in other words, a light saber.

"Take the sword of the Spirit, which is the Word of God" (Ephesians 6:17). "The word of God is sharper than any double-edged sword" (Hebrews 4:12). God's Word is a sword, and at the same time, it's a light. Biblical writers declare, "Your word is a lamp to my feet and a light for my path... The unfolding of your words gives light" (Psalm 119:105). "For these commands are a lamp, this teaching is a light" (Proverbs 6:23). "Pay attention to it as to a light shining in a dark place" (2 Peter 1:19). The Bible is the light saber we need to battle the dark emperor, Satan, and his evil empire.

In some ways, the sword of the Spirit is like some special swords in J.R.R. Tolkien's fantasy epic *The Lord of the Rings*. Frodo the hobbit had a special sword called Sting. When evil orcs were anywhere near, Sting sensed their presence and glowed with bluish light, warning Frodo that an attack was coming. In a similar way, when you have the Holy Spirit and your thinking is in tune with the Bible, the sword of the Spirit detects evil for you. Someone presents a non-biblical teaching, and it just sounds wrong to you—your sword is glowing. Someone suggests a tempting course of action, and it feels wrong to you—your sword is glowing. You can sense when evil is near, even if you can't explain exactly what's wrong. A biblical writer says, "The commands of the Lord are radiant... By them is your servant warned" (Psalm 19:8,11). If anyone is trying to lead you astray, the Holy Spirit's presence and the truth of his Word impressed on your heart keep you from being easily fooled. "The anointing you received from God remains in you, and you do not need anyone to teach you... his anointing teaches you about all things" (1 John 2:26-27). Frodo knew orcs were coming when his sword glowed, and you can know evil is attacking when the sword of the Spirit glows.

The sword of the Spirit doesn't just alert you to evil; it also *defeats* evil. Think of another shining sword in *The Lord of the Rings*, Anduril, the sword of the future king, Aragorn. In Tolkien's words, "The bright blade of Anduril shone like a sudden flame." Long ago, this very sword had cut the ring of power from the hand of the dark lord, Sauron. When the sword was active again in the hand of Aragorn, it meant the dark lord would soon meet his final defeat. As the sword Anduril had a history, so the sword of the Spirit has a history. The sword of Tolkien's tale had defeated the fictional Sauron, but the sword God gives us has defeated Satan himself, who is real and more terrible than any dark lord of fiction. God's Word defeated Satan before—and it will do so again. It is the weapon Satan fears most.

I don't know how much of this Tolkien had in mind when he wrote *The Lord of the Rings*. As a Christian author, he certainly believed in the great conflict between good and evil, but his epic trilogy isn't an allegory. Tolkien didn't mean each detail to have a biblical parallel. Even so, the ability of the sword Sting to detect enemy attackers, and the history of the sword Anduril in defeating the dark lord, can give us hints of what the sword of the Spirit can do in the battle against Satan.

The Master Swordsman

Do you know the power of the sword God has given us? Do you know what mighty victories it has already won? Do you know who used that sword before passing it along to you? The sword God gives us is the very same sword that Jesus used. To know the full value of this sword and to learn how to use it, we should see how the master swordsman has used it.

Just before Jesus began his public ministry, he faced Satan directly. Before he healed others and freed them from demons and brought God's loving reign into their lives, Jesus first had his own showdown with the evil one. Before he helped anyone else, Jesus first proved that he himself could stand up against Satan's temptations and defeat him. How did he succeed? By using the sword of the Spirit! With the Holy Spirit in his heart and the Word of God on his lips, Jesus defeated Satan.

> Jesus, full of the Holy Spirit... was led by the Spirit into the desert, where for forty days he was tempted by the devil. He ate nothing during those days, and at the end of them he was hungry.
>
> The devil said to him, "If you are the Son of God, tell this stone to become bread."
>
> Jesus answered, "It is written: 'Man does not live on bread alone.'"
>
> The devil led him up to a high place and showed him in an instant all the kingdoms of the world. And he said to him, "I will give you all their authority and splendor, for it has been given to me,

and I can give it to anyone I want to. So if you worship me, it will all be yours."

Jesus answered, "It is written: 'Worship the
Lord your God and serve him only.'"

The devil led him to Jerusalem and had him
stand on the highest point of the temple. "If you are
the Son of God," he said, "throw yourself down
from here. For it is written: 'He will command his
angels concerning you to guard you carefully; they
will lift you up in their hands, so that you will not
strike your foot against a stone.'"

Jesus answered, "It says: 'Do not put the Lord
your God to the test.'"

When the devil had finished all this tempting,
he left him until an opportune time. (Luke 4:1-13)
Satan staggered away, defeated by the sword of the Spirit.

Jesus slashed apart all three of Satan's temptations by
quoting the Bible. When Satan tempted Jesus to misuse
miraculous powers for selfish purposes and to put bodily
desires over his relationship to his heavenly Father, Jesus
struck back with, "It is written!" When Satan offered Jesus
a pain-free path to power, telling him he could bypass
God's way of suffering to reclaim the world and could
have world domination simply by honoring Satan instead
of the heavenly Father, Jesus struck back with, "It is written!" Finally, Satan tried to use the Bible itself against Jesus, tempting him to take a suicidal leap and see if biblical
promises of angel protection were really true. But the Bible
is not the sword of Satan; it is the sword of the Spirit. Jesus, full of the Holy Spirit, knew right away that Satan was
misusing Scripture, and Jesus struck back by quoting the
biblical truth which really fit the situation: "Do not put the
Lord your God to the test." All three of Jesus' quotes came
from the Bible book of Deuteronomy. Some of us hardly
know that part of the Bible, but Jesus knew it. Because Jesus knew his Bible so well and because he used it in the

wisdom and strength of the Holy Spirit, he could recognize what was wrong with Satan's temptations and could slash those temptations to pieces. When the Bible says that the Holy Spirit led Jesus into the desert to be tempted by the devil, I've sometimes wondered why the Holy Spirit would put Jesus in such a position. But I've come to understand that the Spirit did it not to endanger Jesus but to deal a blow to Satan and to make Jesus most effective in bringing God's kingdom to others by first winning his own personal battle against Satan. If you are a Spirit-filled follower of Jesus, sometimes the Spirit will do something similar with you: he will lead you into a desert of difficulty and temptation, not to put your soul at risk but to deal a blow to Satan, and to make you most effective in bringing God's kingdom to others by first winning your own personal battle against Satan. You can defeat Satan and make him flee. He will try again some other time, just as he kept watching for other opportunities to tempt Jesus. But if you take God's armor as your protection, and the sword of the Spirit as your ultimate weapon, you can keep driving Satan back.

Jesus, the master swordsman, has beaten Satan and has shown us how it's done. Now he puts the sword in our hand and directs us to use it in the strength of the Holy Spirit. During Jesus' time on earth, he preached the gospel of God's kingdom, healed the sick, and drove out demons—and he wasn't the only one to do those things. Jesus sent his followers to do the same. He started with his inner core, the twelve apostles.

He gave them power and authority to drive out all demons and to cure diseases, and he sent them out to preach the kingdom of God and to heal the sick... So they set out and went from village to village, preaching the gospel and healing people everywhere (Luke 9:1-6).

After this the Lord appointed seventy-two others and sent them two by two ahead of him to every town and place where he was about to go. He told them, "...Heal the sick... and tell them, 'The Kingdom of God is near you' ... he who listens to you listens to me; he who rejects you rejects me; but he who rejects me rejects him who sent me."

The seventy-two returned with joy and said, "Lord, even the demons submit to us in your name."

He replied, "I saw Satan fall like lightning from heaven. I have given you authority to trample on snakes and scorpions and to overcome all the power of the enemy; nothing will harm you. However, do not rejoice that the spirits submit to you, but rejoice that your names are written in heaven (Luke 9:1-16, 10:1-20).

In all of this, Jesus was "full of joy through the Holy Spirit" (Luke 10:21). His friends' names were recorded in God's book of life, and the sword he had put in their hands was defeating the enemy and opening the way for others to enter God's kingdom.

These are not just things that happened long ago. They can keep happening right now. If you follow Jesus and put your confidence in him, the very same Holy Spirit who empowered Jesus and his first missionaries will empower you. The very same sword of the Spirit, the Word of God written in the Bible and spoken in your testimony, is the sword you can use to fight off temptation, make Satan fall with a crash, and win more people and more territory. Jesus, the master swordsman, offers you the very sword he used so successfully against Satan. Become Jesus' apprentice. Learn from the Master how to use this sword most effectively.

A Neglected Weapon

If we take an honest look today at people who own a Bible and say they believe in Jesus, it might not appear that they have the ultimate weapon against evil. Many people who own Bibles are not fighting off Satan or defeating him; instead, Satan is defeating them. Is that because the Bible isn't a strong enough weapon? No, it's because people aren't using it. The Bible isn't a weak weapon; it's a neglected weapon. If you own a Bible but lay it on a shelf and don't use it, and then go into a sin-dominated world without God's Word as your weapon, it's like walking into the enemy camp and laying your weapon down. The army of the Lord has the ultimate weapon, the sword of the Spirit, and we can't afford to lay that weapon down. But that's what far too many people are doing.

Nowhere in the world do more people own Bibles than in North America. But in most of the homes, the Bible stays on the shelf, with the result that Satan is defeating many Americans and Canadians. The level of divorce, despair, pornography, selfishness, greed, addiction, error, and violence is high in these countries where so many own Bibles and call themselves Christians. Polls find that most Canadians and Americans believe in God and in Jesus as the Son of God. God may be doing well in polls, but polls don't amount to much in spiritual warfare. Replying to a survey is one thing; defeating Satan is quite another. Many Canadians and Americans believe in Jesus and own Bibles, but far fewer are triumphing over Satan, overcoming temptation, discipling others, and making their culture more Christ-like. A huge part of the reason for this failure is that most are not using the sword of the Spirit. They own Bibles but don't read them. They consider themselves part of a church, but seldom attend or hear biblical preaching.

Of the huge number of American teenagers who say they are Christians, two out of three think Satan is not a real being but just a symbol of evil. Over half say Jesus committed sins while he was on earth. What confusion! How can Jesus be divine and still commit sins? How can anyone claim to take the Bible seriously and yet say that Satan is only a symbol? Such ideas would sound ridiculous to anyone who really knows the Bible, but many who claim Christianity are almost clueless about what the Bible actually says. Most people own Bibles, but how many really read the Bible and believe it and see it as the ultimate weapon in a war against a deadly, demonic enemy? We have the sword of the Spirit, but we have no idea how to use it against Satan because we don't know the Scripture, and we don't recognize the enemy.

The problem is not a shortage of Bibles but a shortage of Bible *reading* and biblical *living*. As fewer people read the Bible at home, and as fewer churches uphold biblical truth, they become spiritually weaker. Their marriages become less stable, their children become more prone to trouble and less interested in church, and various other problems become more frequent. If more people would live by God's Word and bring it to others, the result would be more divine blessing and fewer casualties of Satan's attacks.

Churches and denominations that neglect biblical doctrines and morality have mostly been shrinking, while those that teach biblical truth and high standards of holiness are attracting people. Those who neglect the sword of the Spirit are losing, while those who use the sword are advancing in the battle against sin and Satan. This is true not just in North America but in Africa and in every other part of the world. Countless people claim to be Christians, but only those who faithfully read the Bible and live by the Spirit can overcome Satan and live differently from the world around them.

Fight with Confidence

When I mention the widespread neglect of Scripture, I'm not just saying, "Naughty, naughty! Shame on you for not reading your Bible more often!" Reading your Bible is not a matter of doing your homework to get a gold star from your teacher. It is a matter of using your light saber to fight off the enemy and drive him back. My main concern is that so many people are losing to Satan when they could be winning. Retreat and defeat could turn to victory if only they would start using the sword of the Spirit.

Let's forget the polls and surveys and talk about you. How often do you read the Bible? How well do you know it? Do you know specific truths that drive back error and fight off temptation? If the Son of God himself depended on Scripture to fight Satan, how can you possibly fight Satan without it? Take up the sword. Get a grip on your light saber. Read your Bible faithfully—not just weekly, but daily. Listen to the Bible preached faithfully in church. The better your grip on the sword of the Spirit, the more you can defeat Satan. Husbands and wives who read the Bible and pray together daily almost never get divorced. Children who are trained each day in God's Word are much less likely to fall into Satan's clutches. Sin isn't just a matter of naughtiness and guilt. Sin wounds and wrecks your life. And God's Word is the ultimate weapon against sin. As a biblical writer puts it, "I have hidden your word in my heart that I might not sin against you" (Psalm 119:11). So arm yourself and your family and your friends with the ultimate weapon. If you have a Bible, use it!

When you fight Satan, use the very sword Jesus used. Fight in the power of the very Spirit who empowered Jesus. The Bible is the sword of the Spirit because the Holy Spirit produced it, the Holy Spirit guides you in how to use it, and the Holy Spirit energizes it and makes it effective. The Bible "never had its origins in the will of man, but men spoke from God as they were carried along *by the Ho-*

ly Spirit" (2 Peter 1:21). The Holy Spirit made this sword,
and the Holy Spirit teaches you to use it. Without the Spirit
of God, you can't understand the things of God, and you
can't put his weapon to good use. But the Spirit gives you
"the mind of Christ" (2 Corinthians 2:11-16). The Spirit
brings alive the words of the Bible, enabling you to think
like Jesus, understand spiritual truth as Jesus does, and to
defeat Satan as Jesus did. And when Satan attacks, the
mighty, limitless power of the Spirit enters your sword,
defeating Satan and destroying his strongholds. "The
weapons we fight with are not the weapons of the world.
On the contrary, they have divine power to demolish
strongholds. We demolish arguments and every pretension
that sets itself up against the knowledge of God, and we
take captive every thought to make it obedient to Christ" (2
Corinthians 10:4-5). The gospel is the power of God for
defeating Satan and bringing salvation to all who believe
(Romans 1:18).

When you use the sword of the Spirit, the Holy Spirit
may lead you into some hard situations, just as he led Jesus
into the desert to be tempted by Satan. The Spirit may do
this to help you prove your strength and grow toward maturity.

I read about a village in which a boy would be considered a man when he turned thirteen. On the night of his
thirteenth birthday, some villagers would blindfold the boy
and lead him far into the forest. When the blindfold was
removed, the boy would find himself alone in total darkness. There he would spend the night. Unable to see much
of anything, he might hear the howl of a wolf, the growl of
a bear, the snarl of a mountain lion. He might hear twigs
cracking and branches snapping nearby and not know what
sort of enemy or predator might be approaching. Then, as
dawn got closer and the light increased, he would begin to
see the green of leaves and the color of flowers. And then
he would see something else: a strong man, a heavily

armed warrior, standing guard a short distance away. It was his father. The father had been there all along, ready to defend his son from any dangers that lurked in the dark. The boy became a man by going through the danger, but even as a man, he was still not alone. He had a guard and defender.

You may go through something similar. You may feel alone, surrounded by the powers of darkness. That can be scary, but it can also be an opportunity for greater maturity. As the Bible says, "Be on your guard, stand firm in the faith, act like men, be strong" (1 Corinthians 16:13 NASB). But even as you grow stronger, more mature, more skilled in using your sword, the Holy Spirit is right there, beside you and within you. That's all the more reason to live with confidence and to fight with confidence. The Spirit not only gives you the ultimate weapon; he himself is the ultimate friend and defender.

Chapter Sixteen

Warrior Prayer

And pray in the Spirit on all occasions with all kinds of prayers and requests. With this in mind, be alert and always keep on praying for all the saints. (Ephesians 6:18)

Napoleon once said, "An army marches on its stomach." He didn't mean that soldiers always crawl on their bellies. He meant that troops need good meals in their stomachs in order to march to victory. No matter how brilliant the generals, no matter how brave the soldiers, they can't win battles if they are starving or freezing. Troops need food and other supplies.

Napoleon knew this, but a shortage of supplies still turned out to be his downfall. In 1812, he invaded Russia with a huge army, larger than anyone had ever seen. As Napoleon advanced, the Russians did little to stop him. Rather than fight a head-on battle, the Russians kept retreating. As they retreated, they left nothing behind for the invading army to use as supplies. The farther Napoleon advanced into Russia, the longer the supply lines became. Small groups of Russians kept attacking the supply lines at various points.

Eventually the supply lines were so long and so unreliable that Napoleon's army faced devastating shortages. There was a shortage of food, and many of the soldiers suffered from lack of nourishment. There was a shortage of medical supplies and bandages, and many perished from lack of proper treatment. There was a shortage of clothing and fuel for fires and heating, and when the terrible Russian winter struck, many of Napoleon's men shivered and died of hypothermia and cold-related diseases. For every man who died in battle, five died of other causes, mostly due to shortages of supplies. Napoleon had to leave Russia, his army in tatters.

In 1941, another dictator decided to invade Russia. Adolph Hitler had easily conquered most of Europe already, and his army seemed unbeatable. Hitler invaded Russia with an army even larger than Napoleon's had been—more than three million soldiers, with thousands of tanks, artillery, and aircraft. Hitler's forces advanced swiftly, and the Russians retreated, leaving little the Germans could use for food and supplies. The farther the German army moved into Russia, the longer the supply lines became. Winter came. Russian snipers kept attacking the German lines of supply and communication. Hitler's troops lacked food, fuel, and winter clothing. Finally, after terrible losses on both sides, the Russian forces defeated the weakened German troops and drove them back.

"An army marches on its stomach." Military campaigns depend on supplies. That's true in spiritual warfare as well: you need a constant flow of supplies. When you're fighting Satan, you need to be strong, brave, and well equipped with God's armor and weapons, but you also need nourishment to keep up your energy. You need good supply lines.

Supply Line

What's your spiritual supply line? What connects you with headquarters? Prayer. Prayer is the line between you and God. It is through prayer that God supplies your daily needs. It is through prayer that you get refreshed and reenergized for serving Jesus and battling Satan.

In Ephesians 6, the Bible calls God's people to combat and presents various pieces of spiritual armor and weaponry. But it doesn't stop there. Ephesians 6:18 goes on to say, "And pray in the Spirit on all occasions with all kinds of prayers and requests. With this in mind, be alert and always keep on praying for all the saints." Prayer is the way to get fresh supplies, inner nourishment, and everything necessary for a soldier of Jesus to stay healthy and strong in spirit.

When we pray, we are getting supplies from divine headquarters. God has no shortage of resources to draw from. Earlier in Ephesians, the apostle Paul says that God "is able to do immeasurably more than all we ask or imagine" (Ephesians 3:20). There is no need too great for God to meet, no prayer too big for God to answer. God never runs out of resources. The Bible says, "God is able to make all grace to abound to you, so that in all things at all times, having all that you need, you will abound in every good work" (2 Corinthians 9:8). If I suffer a spiritual shortage, the problem is not that headquarters has no more supplies to send me. The problem is that the supply lines are interrupted by failure of prayer.

Satan will do all he can to hinder your prayers. He doesn't have to defeat you in direct combat if he can manage to starve your soul by cutting off any prayer connection with God. Satan can use a method similar to what the Russians did against Napoleon. Russian fighters were often busier interrupting the supply lines than trying to take on the main army. Likewise, Satan may find it more effective not to confront you directly with a huge temptation or a terrible tragedy. He may simply attack your supply line and keep you from prayer. If he succeeds in doing that, your defeat will be only a matter of time.

Maybe you have no interest in prayer. In that case, you have no relationship with God, and you're not in his army at all. You're not a soldier for Christ; you're in the realm controlled by Satan. The devil already has you where he wants you, and if you never start praying, you'll remain far from God and under Satan's domination. One of the first signs of salvation, one of the first marks of spiritual life, is prayer, real communication with God. The apostle Paul was once a murderer and an enemy of Jesus. When Jesus transformed Paul, the Lord sent another Christian to help Paul. What did Jesus tell this person to indicate that Paul was a new person, no longer enslaved by Satan? Jesus said, "Behold, he is praying" (Acts 9:11).

Spiritual life begins in prayer, and it is sustained through prayer. To be a Christian is to have God's life in your inner being. The more the Holy Spirit fills you with life and power, the more energy you have to defend yourself against Satan, march forward against him, and rescue others from his wicked reign. Prayer nourishes and strengthens the Spirit-life within you. This inner nourishment, this filling by the Holy Spirit, is not automatic. It comes in answer to prayer. God is a loving Father, willing and able to keep filling your inner being with more and more of his life, but this won't happen without prayer. To those who are suffering from spiritual shortages, the Bible says, "You do not have, because you do not ask God" (James 4:2). Jesus says, "Your Father in heaven will give the Holy Spirit to those who *ask* him" (Luke 11:13). Prayer is your supply line. It's the way to receive God's resources. You can't battle Satan if your inner self is empty and starving. Wherever you go, whatever you do, maintain the supply lines. "Pray in the Spirit on all occasions with all kinds of prayers and requests" (Ephesians 6:18). "Pray without ceasing" (1 Thessalonians 5:17).

Prayer is the way spiritual warriors get supplies from heavenly headquarters. Racing into new situations without prayer is like launching a military invasion without any supply lines. You can try lots of things, pour your effort and energy into them, and end up feeling weak and empty inside. This is true of any warrior who fails to pray, and it's especially true for leaders. If you're a pastor, an elder, or a teacher, you may be very skilled and have some excellent ideas. You may be like an elite soldier with superb training, the finest protection, the latest weaponry, and the most brilliant strategy. But how many victories can you win if you're starving?

Without prayer, your inner being becomes emptier, weaker and more famished, and you end up in defeat. Some church leaders fall into scandal. Others don't do anything awful; they just quit the ministry in discouragement and despair. When do leaders become most vulnerable to scandalous behavior? Often it's after they've poured their energy into all sorts of people and projects without taking the time to renew their own souls through prayer and communion with God. What causes some leaders to burn out, give up, and quit their calling? Often it's not a lack of talent or training or accomplishment but because they neglect their own spirit for too long and don't maintain their supply line with God's Holy Spirit. Long before Satan attacks with a particular scandalous temptation or an overwhelming feeling of despair, he may first be busy attacking supply lines, keeping you from connecting with God through prayer.

Keep the supply line open. "Pray in the Spirit on all occasions." Stay in touch with God. Let his Spirit nourish your spirit. Then you will be able to resist temptation and discouragement, and you can help those around you. As the Bible says, "I can do all things through Him who strengthens me... And my God shall supply all your needs according to his riches in glory in Christ Jesus" (Philippians 4:19 NASB). When you have that kind of supply line, you can feast on God's goodness and rejoice in him. This is the nourishment you need to stay strong against Satan.

Line of Communication

Prayer is our supply line. It's also our line of communication. Communication is vital to any relationship, and especially for our relationship with God. In prayer we converse with God as our Father and Friend, but here I want to emphasize warrior prayer: communicating with the Lord as our supreme commander.

A military force needs excellent communication and coordination in order to win battles. Soldiers must know what their commanders want. Generals must know where attacks are coming from, where reinforcements are needed, and how each unit is progressing. In spiritual warfare, prayer is the way we stay in touch with headquarters and coordinate our own efforts with the Lord's battle plan.

If you are a soldier for Jesus, he doesn't want you racing around, fighting here and there, without knowing your orders. You need your commander's direction so that you serve his strategy. In other words, you need his wisdom. How can you get it? The Bible says, "If any of you lacks wisdom, he should ask God, who gives generously to all without finding fault, and it will be given to him" (James 1:5). To get God's wisdom and guidance, just ask! Pray! Your commander won't scold you for asking. He'll guide you and direct you where he wants you to be. He provides basic training and overall guidance through the Bible, and when you need special guidance for a particular situation, his Spirit will impress on your spirit the wisest course of action. But this isn't automatic. You must ask. You must "pray in the Spirit on all occasions." The more you communicate with God, the more he will communicate with you and let you know what he wants you to do next.

You can communicate with headquarters to find out what God wants, and you can also pray to tell God what you need. This gives you a huge advantage in spiritual warfare. Sometimes you may feel overwhelmed by Satan's forces. You feel surrounded with no way out. But you can still pray. You can call headquarters for an air strike. Soldiers who are backed by superior air power aren't necessarily defeated just because their unit is outgunned and outmaneuvered on the ground. They can radio for extra help, and within minutes, fighter jets or attack helicopters swoop in to deal with the enemy. Even if you're a lowly foot soldier in God's army, air support is only a prayer away. God can send extra angels to your defense, and he can direct his own vast power against the evil forces that have you pinned down.

In Exodus 17, the Bible describes a battle between God's people, the Israelites, and their mortal enemies, the Amalekites. The Israelite soldiers under Joshua marched against the enemy, while Moses went to the top of a hill to pray. "As long as Moses held up his hands [in prayer], the Israelites were winning, but whenever he lowered his hands, the Amalekites were winning" (Exodus 17:12). The soldiers on the ground could win only with air support from heaven. When Moses got too tired to hold up his hands, two other men supported him. "Aaron and Hur held his hands up—one on one side, one on the other—so that his hands remained steady till sunset" (17:13). That enabled God's people to defeat their enemies.

Victory depends on prayer. Why? Because victory depends on God. Jesus tells us, "Without me you can do nothing" (John 15:5). The apostle Paul, who wrote Ephesians 6 and knew so much about spiritual warfare, knew that on his own, he didn't have what it took to carry out his mission. Paul said, "Our sufficiency is of God" (2 Corinthians 3:5 KJV).

A man once asked Jesus' disciples to drive a demon out of his son. The disciples had already succeeded in driving out some other demons, but they were not able to drive this one out. Then Jesus came on the scene, and he succeeded in making the demon leave. Later, his disciples asked him privately, "Why couldn't we drive it out?" Jesus replied, "This kind can come out only by prayer" (Mark 9:28-29).

That's true of many enemies we face and of many problems we have: *this kind can be dealt with only by prayer.* There may be some things we can deal with simply by using strength God has already given us, but some enemies are so strong that we need more power than we've received thus far. The way to get that power is prayer. When the enemy is too much for you, use your line of communication to call headquarters for more air support.

Praying for All the Saints

Prayer is the line of supply and communication for each individual soldier of Christ, and remember: you're not the only soldier in the struggle. If you're a Christian, you're part of an army. You should care not just about yourself but about your fellow warriors in the struggle against Satan. What happens to any part of the church affects the whole church (1 Corinthians 12:26). If you succeed against Satan, it helps your fellow soldiers; if they succeed, it helps you. If you fail, it hurts their position; if they fail, it hurts you. The apostle Paul says, "Who is weak, and I do not feel weak? Who is led into sin, and I do not inwardly burn?" (2 Corinthians 11:29). In the Lord's army, it's all for one, and one for all. So when you pray, don't just pray for yourself. Pray for all who are fighting for the Lord along with you. "Always keep on praying for all the saints." (Ephesians 6:18) Don't just pray for your own congregation or denomination. Pray for the church of Jesus all around the world.

Sometimes, when someone is going through a time of terrible stress or suffering, they find it hard to pray. Their mind is spinning, their spirit is exhausted, and they've already prayed so much they feel prayed out. But even if they're so overwhelmed they can hardly pray, you can pray for them. A number of Christians who have gone through hard times have told me what a comfort it was to know that even when they couldn't pray, others were praying for them, and God was hearing those prayers. Part of spiritual warfare is being alert not only to Satan's attacks on you but his attacks on others, and praying not only for yourself but for those who are facing the fiercest attacks.

When you pray for others, it's good for them, and it's good for you. One of the worst problems for many of us today is just plain self-centeredness. It's possible to be so focused on *my* health, *my* success, *my* looks, *my* reputation, *my* spiritual standing that it makes me sick in spirit. If all I think about is me, me, me, and if all I pray about is me, me, me, it makes me spiritually unhealthy. Many individuals and churches could get beyond petty problems if only they would recognize the huge threat of Satan, trust the power of God, and pray for each other and for all the saints and for the advance of God's kingdom, rather than centering on themselves.

Pray for all the saints. Pray for young Christians who are surrounded by more temptations than any generation of youth in history. Pray for Christian parents who aren't sure they're up to the challenge of bringing up children. Pray for single Christians who struggle with loneliness. Pray for middle-aged Christians who wonder if their life counts for much. Pray for elderly Christians who are in failing health and may face cruel demonic attacks of doubt and fear as death comes closer.

Pray for all the saints. Pray for Christian teachers who mentor children. Pray for Christians in business who struggle to be honest. Pray for Christian farmers and factory workers, Christian lawyers, doctors, and other professionals, who struggle to apply their faith to their profession. Pray for all Christians everywhere who must shine for Christ while fighting off Satan's attacks.

Pray for all the saints, especially for those who are persecuted or in prison. The Bible says, "Remember those in prison as if you were their fellow prisoners, and those who are mistreated as if you yourselves were suffering" (Hebrews 13:3). Many persecuted Christians say that this is what they want most: to be remembered, to be prayed for, to know that they are not abandoned by God or forgotten by fellow believers.

Praying for Church Leaders

Please pray also for pastors and missionaries. When Paul told the Ephesians to pray for all the saints, he added, "Pray also for me, that whenever I open my mouth, words may be given me that I may fearlessly make known the mystery of the gospel, for which I am an ambassador in chains. Pray that I may declare it fearlessly, as I should" (6:19-20). If this mighty man of God asked people to pray for him, then surely your pastor needs your prayers. Other Christian leaders need your prayers. A preacher's effectiveness doesn't depend just on his talent or even on his own prayers but on the prayers of his people. Someone once asked British preacher Charles Spurgeon the secret of his success in winning so many thousands to Christ. Spurgeon replied, "My people pray for me."

What should you pray for? What should you ask God to do for preachers and leaders? Pray that God will give them a message and the boldness to speak that message clearly. That's what Paul wanted. He was in prison, but he didn't ask the Ephesians to pray for his freedom. He was in poor health, but he didn't ask them to pray that he would thrive and prosper. Paul asked them to pray that he would be able to proclaim Christ fearlessly.

I always feel encouraged when someone says, "I pray for you." Like Paul, I especially appreciate prayers that God will give me words and make me fearless. Do you know how hard it can be for a preacher to prepare a message and to come up with the right words? Do you know how hard it is to be bold? I'm timid by nature. Boldness doesn't come naturally to me. I like to get along with people. I don't like to offend anyone. And yet if I speak God's message, some will be offended. I need prayers that I will be free from worry about human opinion and simply speak God's message boldly, whatever the reaction might be.

For some pastors, it's more dangerous to be bold than it is for me. Some may have their freedom and life endangered if government officials oppose their message. Others may have their income and position endangered if a wealthy member of their congregation is offended and wants the pastor out and withholds money. Other pastors may just get so worn down in spirit that they run out of lively words and have no energy left to be bold. When they get up and preach, it's because they have to say something, not because they have something to say. They need words from God and boldness from God. Their own prayer life may get dangerously weak, but if fellow believers stand with them and pray for them, the Lord can make them strong and bold again.

The church desperately needs pastors and leaders who preach God's Word plainly and send his battle signal loud and clear. "If the trumpet does not sound a clear call, who will get ready for battle?" (1 Corinthians 14:8). So pray for preachers. Pray that they will have boldness to sound God's trumpet! Pray that they will speak the truth as they should: fearlessly, truthfully, lovingly, and effectively.

We're in a war. Satan and his evil forces are trying to destroy us. So be strong in the Lord and in the power of his might. Put on the full armor of God. Use the ultimate weapon against Satan, the sword of the Spirit, the Word of God. And don't neglect your lines of supply and communication. Pray in the Spirit on all occasions.

Epilogue

A Winning Spirit

For the Spirit God gave us does not make us timid, but gives us power, love and self-control. (2 Timothy 1:7)

In spiritual warfare, you need the heart of an eagle, not the heart of a chicken. Eagles are bold and strong and soar in the heavens. "Chicken" is the nickname you get if you're timid and cowardly. Chickens don't soar. They weigh too much. Worry and fear make them too heavy to fly upward. But if you're a daring eagle, your spirit is lighter and your wings are stronger. If you want to soar to new levels, be an eagle, not a chicken. A chicken has a losing spirit; an eagle has a winning spirit. What does a winning spirit have that a losing spirit lacks? At least three things: power, love, and self-control.

First, a winning spirit has *power*, while a losing spirit doesn't. A losing spirit feels like a victim. Everything seems to be against you, and you don't have the strength to deal with it. A losing spirit expects to fail. But a winning spirit expects to succeed. A winning spirit may face big challenges, but it draws on a source of inner strength more powerful than anything that is against you. It's a spirit of power.

Second, a winning spirit has *love*; a losing spirit lacks it. A losing spirit feels forsaken, lonely, mistreated, unloved. Feeling so unloved, a losing spirit can't give love in a healthy way or build solid relationships. A winning spirit, on the other hand, feels cherished, embraced, blessed, loved. A winning spirit—secure in being loved with enormous, unending love—is eager to expand the circle of love and builds loving, flourishing relationships with others. It's a spirit of love.

Third, a winning spirit has *self-control*; a losing spirit feels out of control. A losing spirit feels dominated by unchangeable situations and uncontrollable urges, panicking or acting foolishly on impulse or behaving rashly. A winning spirit can handle any challenge with a sense of calm and purpose. It keeps a level head and makes choices based on what's best, not based on panic or impulse. It's a spirit of self-control.

Are you an eagle with a winning spirit of power, love, and self-control? Or are you a chicken with a losing spirit? It's no fun to have that chicken feeling, and it's not how you're meant to live. Maybe you feel stuck with a losing spirit. How can you get rid of it? How can you have a winning spirit instead? Well, don't just try to think positive. Don't just work on being a little braver or having a brighter outlook. Trying to give yourself a winning spirit won't work. If you're a chicken, it won't help much to decide that from now on you are going to fly high in the sky. Chickens can flap their wings and even get off the ground for a few moments, but they always come back down with a thud. If you're a chicken, you can try to fly, you can try to change your attitude and make yourself into the person you want to be, but do-it-yourself efforts to make a losing spirit act like a winning spirit end with a thud.

If you want a winning spirit, don't depend on your own weak spirit. We're all chickens at heart. The sooner we admit it, the better. We lack power. We lack love. We lack self-control. To soar like an eagle, we need to give up on our own timid spirit and seek a spirit greater than our own, the Holy Spirit of the Lord Jesus Christ. The Bible says that in our own power, even the strongest of us eventually stumble and run out of energy, "but those who hope in the

Lord will renew their strength. They will soar on wings like eagles" (Isaiah 40:31).

You need to have God's Holy Spirit in you, and you need to be aware of the transforming effect he has on your spirit. "For the Spirit God gave us does not make us timid, but gives us power, love and self-control" (2 Timothy 1:7).

Spirit of Power

In order to have a winning spirit like an eagle, you need power: power to deal with challenges, power to overcome discouragement, power to resist temptation, power to handle any situation life throws at you. You need power not just to survive but to thrive, not just to defend yourself but to go on the offensive and move forward. To win in spiritual warfare, you need the kind of power the apostle Paul spoke of when he said, "I can do everything through him who gives me strength" (Philippians 4:13).

An eagle's winning spirit exclaims, "I can do everything!" But a chicken's losing spirit moans, "I can't do anything." It's awful to have a victim mentality. The victim mentality comes in many forms. You were abused as a child, so you're worthless and will never amount to anything. Or you've plunged into drinking and drugs, and nothing can break your addiction. Or your marriage and family life is a mess, and there's no way you'll ever enjoy positive, joyful relationships. Or you've lost your job, and you don't have what it takes to succeed in today's world. Or you've done something so awful that God can't possibly forgive you or love you. You're dirt. You're helpless. You're hopeless. What's the use of trying to move ahead? You're going to fail anyway. You're just a chicken headed for slaughter.

I hear various people who talk that way. I hear defeat in their voices. I see despair in their eyes. As they tell of their troubles and how grim the future looks, it makes me sad, and it makes me mad. It makes me sad that they feel so hopeless, and it makes me mad that Satan has been lying to them.

Satan wants us to think that there's no way to overcome the forces that are against us. Satan wants us to believe that sin, sadness, failure, and death are all that the future holds. But Satan is a liar! He wants you to feel helpless and to think there's no way you can win. But that's a lie.

The truth is this. Satan doesn't have a chance against the power of God. Satan is stronger than we are on our own, but Satan and all his demons combined have no chance against even one person who has the power of God's Holy Spirit. The only way Satan can keep you down is to feed you lies.

Satan may start by telling you the lie that you can do just fine on your own without God. You feel smart, strong, and sure to succeed. Who needs God? But at some point, that lie usually gets exposed. Your life starts crumbling. It becomes obvious that you can't make it on your own. At that point, Satan switches to a new lie. He says you're a loser, you'll always be a loser, you have no chance to ever be anything or do anything. Just accept that you're a chicken doomed to be devoured.

Satan tries to bury you in such lies so that you won't focus on the fact that God is far more powerful than Satan and so that you'll never connect with God's power through faith. The moment you start believing in God's power and sense his power at work in you, Satan hasn't got a chance. Satan trying to beat God is like a mosquito trying to beat a tiger. By faith in God's power, you can walk all over Satan (Romans 16:20), and he knows it. Nothing frightens the devil more than faith. The devil trembles every time a person rejects his lies, believes in the almighty strength of the living God, and stands against Satan by the power of the Holy Spirit.

If you put your faith in Jesus and have the Holy Spirit living in you, then you have power inside you greater than any power in all the world, greater than the power of Satan himself. The Bible says to Christians, "You, dear children, are from God and have overcome them, because the one who is in you is greater than the one who is in the world" (1 John 4:4). How can you put God's power into action in your fight against Satan? By faith. By faith reject Satan's lies. By faith believe God's truth in Christ. "This is the victory that has overcome the world, even our faith. Who is it that overcomes the world? Only he who believes that Jesus is the Son of God" (1 John 5:4-5).

Faith is the way to receive forgiveness of sins and eternal life, and faith is also the way to defeat Satan and his schemes.

Faith in Jesus is the pipeline through which the power of the Holy Spirit flows. The Holy Spirit's power is the very same power by which Jesus did his miracles. Jesus preached the gospel in the power of the Holy Spirit. Jesus cast out demons in the power of the Holy Spirit. Jesus gave sight to the blind and hearing to the deaf by the power of the Holy Spirit. Jesus made lame people walk and paralyzed people dance by the power of the Holy Spirit. Jesus even raised dead people to life by the power of the Holy Spirit. In fact, it was the power of the Holy Spirit that raised Jesus himself from the grave and gave him the decisive victory over death, sin, and Satan.

All these miracles were astonishing, but just as astonishing is the miracle Christ does every time he takes a soul dead in sin and brings it to life by his Spirit. Still today the Holy Spirit drives out demons and sets people free from Satan. Still today the Holy Spirit smashes barriers and brings healing and wholeness. Still today the Holy Spirit fills individuals and transforms families. Still today the Spirit transforms earthbound chickens into soaring eagles.

Still today the Holy Spirit brings the resurrection power of Christ into the lives of ordinary people.

Jesus Christ has almighty power, and that same power is in our hearts if we have his Holy Spirit living in us. Some religions are mostly rituals and words without life or power, but real faith in the living Lord Jesus is much more than that. "The kingdom of God is not a matter of talk but of power" (1 Corinthians 4:20).

This power is a great protection. If you trust the risen Christ and have his Spirit living in you, then you "by faith are shielded by God's power" (1 Peter 1:5). This shield isn't just something you have; it is something you must use. "Take up the shield of faith, with which you can extinguish all the flaming arrows of the evil one" (Ephesians 6:16).

You're not just up against unpleasant things or vague forces. You are up against personal, hateful spirits of wickedness, led by Satan himself. Satan will keep shooting fiery darts at you, but don't be afraid. Faith is fireproof. With every new attack of Satan, take up your faith afresh. You will be shielded by God's power from whatever Satan does. The devil wants you to think he can't be beat, but the Holy Spirit inside you is greater than the devil outside you. Faith will give you victory even if Satan and the whole world are against you.

All of us need this encouragement, even Christian leaders—especially Christian leaders! No one faces fiercer attacks from Satan than those of us who have a special calling to lead others in faith. We can get discouraged about our own sins and limited abilities. We can get disappointed by a church that seems stuck in a rut or a community that doesn't seem responsive to the gospel. We can get disheartened by results that fall short of our hopes. We can get disoriented and deceived by sly lies that Satan tells through scholars who deny or distort the Bible. We can become doubtful, timid, tired. We can wonder why we're in the ministry at all. We can wonder whether there's any point in following Jesus.

But, fellow leader, don't give up! Don't be afraid! "The Spirit that God has given us does not make us timid; instead, his Spirit fills us with power, love, and self-control" (2 Timothy 1:7 TEV). Those words from God were first given to encourage a *pastor*. Young pastor Timothy tended to be timid, so the apostle Paul encouraged him. We leaders need to encourage each other and remind each other what sort of Spirit God has given us—not a timid spirit, but the mighty Holy Spirit of Christ himself.

If you're a Christian and have the Holy Spirit living in you, then be bold! Be strong! Be courageous! Be fiercely glad! Don't let Satan's attacks get you down. Every new attack you face is an opportunity to win another victory. When Satan attacks you, attack right back. Don't let his attacks frighten you. Let them gladden you. If Satan is firing volley after volley of flaming arrows at you, it means he's worried about you. You're a threat to him. Be glad about that.

"Resist the devil, and he will flee from you" (James 4:7). Fight in the Spirit's power, and you will win. Satan wants to scare you with the lie that he's winning, but the truth is that he's already lost. Christ is on the throne, and he gives believers the Spirit of power.

Spirit of Love

Along with power, another life-changing blessing of the Holy Spirit is love. Nothing in all the world matters so much as knowing you are loved and being able to love others. The Bible says those who trust Christ are able to rejoice even in troubles and have bright hope for the future, "because God has poured out his love into our hearts by the Holy Spirit" (Romans 5:5).

God showed his great love in sending his Son, Jesus, to die for us while we were still ungodly sinners and enemies of the Lord (Romans 5:8). Jesus' death on the cross was a once-for-all payment more than sufficient to cover the sins of the world. If God loved us so much when we were enemies fighting against him, what can stop him from loving us once he has made us his friends? One of the main works of the Holy Spirit is simply to seal God's love on our hearts.

I am amazed anew every time I see the change that occurs in people who really begin to know in their hearts that God loves them. Their hard and rebellious exterior softens and melts. Their sense of being rotten and unlovable gives way to the joy and warmth of being treasured by God. Self-destructive addictions and suicidal thoughts begin to shrink and a new will to live takes over. In some cases the change is sudden and striking. In other cases it occurs over a period of time, with many ups and downs. But the change is unmistakable. The love of God may pour in with a rush, or it may trickle in slowly and secretly, but the result is the same: a heart filled with God's love.

Once the love of God flows into you, God's love also begins to flow from you to others. I have seen women who were once wicked become some of the most faithful wives and tender mothers I know, thanks to God's love. I have seen men who were harsh and selfish become caring husbands and wise, affectionate fathers, thanks to God's love. I have seen couples on the verge of divorce renewed in love for each other after God's love came into their lives, thanks to God's love. I have seen slaves of drugs and alcohol set free and made active in bringing freedom to others, thanks to God's love. I have seen greedy, hard-hearted workaholics become kind and generous, thanks to God's love. I have seen suicidal, hateful teens become hopeful and helpful, thanks to God's love. I have seen criminals who grew up in loveless homes and did dreadful deeds become eager to rescue others from Satan's hate and lies, thanks to God's love. Nothing is more deadly than to be a hater who feels hated, and nothing is more life-changing than to be a lover who feels loved.

Sometimes, though, even followers of Jesus forget how much they are loved and may fail to love others. They become fearful in their own hearts and harsh in their attitudes toward others. The Bible tells of a time when a village didn't welcome Jesus and his disciples because of racial and political prejudice. That made Jesus' followers furious. "When the disciples James and John saw this, they asked, 'Lord, do you want us to call fire down from heaven to destroy them?' But Jesus turned and rebuked them, and they went to another village" (John 9:45-56).

Some ancient Bible manuscripts say that when Jesus rebuked them, he said, "You do not know what kind of spirit you are of, for the Son of Man did not come to destroy men's lives, but to save them." If you want God to blast your enemies instantly, you're not in tune with the Holy Spirit of Christ. He's not the Spirit of hatred and instant payback; he's the Spirit of love, patience, and another chance.

If that's not our attitude toward others, if we have a harsh and vengeful attitude toward them, it may mean that we ourselves aren't yet feeling secure in God's love. "Righteous anger" can be a mask for inner anguish. A cold, cruel attitude toward others may flow from a lack of faith in God's love for us. Even if we belong to him, we may still lack full assurance and experience of his love, and that can poison our behavior toward others and rob us of the joy God wants us to have. The Bible says repeatedly that the Holy Spirit replaces fear with love. "There is no fear in love. But perfect love drives out fear, because fear has to do with punishment. The one who fears is not made perfect in love" (1 John 4:18). "Those who are led by the Spirit of God are sons of God. For you did not receive a spirit that makes you a slave again to fear, but you received the Spirit of sonship. And by him we cry, "Abba, Father.""

The Spirit himself testifies with our spirit that we are God's children" (Romans 8:14-16).

Do you know in your spirit that you are a dearly loved child of God because of Jesus Christ? Has the Holy Spirit flooded your heart with so much of God's love that fear has been forced out? You will feel like a chicken, a loser, as long as you fear that nobody really loves you—at least nobody who knows what you are really like. But if you know that God loves you fully and forever, even though he knows every bad thing you've done and the evil that still lurks in your heart, then God's love gives you a winning spirit, a spirit that soars on eagle's wings.

Spirit of Self-Control

A third blessing of the Holy Spirit, along with power and love, is self-control. In fact, power and love are the key to self-control.

The Spirit's power builds self-control by preventing you from panicking and losing control in the face of things that are happening around you. Knowing you have inner power to win, you stay calm at the center and enjoy peace that surpasses understanding. You master the situation; the situation doesn't master you. God's power enables you to control yourself.

The Spirit's love builds self-control by giving you a sound mind, a healthy realism, a stable personality. Out-of-control people are often driven by hatred or by a desperate craving for love that has never been satisfied. Serious lack of self-control appears in various forms—alcoholism, drug addiction, eating problems, sexual compulsions, obsession with work, inability to control anger—but whatever the form, these problems usually arise in a spirit starved for love. Once that craving is satisfied by the Holy Spirit pouring God's love into your heart, the old urges no longer dominate. God's love puts you in your right mind and gives you self-control.

Do you have a winning spirit? Do you have the power, love, and self-control that enable you to soar like an eagle? Only the Holy Spirit can make that a reality for you. Only the Spirit can get you off the ground, and only the Spirit can keep you soaring. As the Bible puts it, "this all-surpassing power is from God and not from us" (2 Corinthians 4:7). The Spirit God gave us does not make us timid, but gives us power, love and self-control. Only in the Spirit's strength can you follow Jesus to victory over the devil, the world, and the flesh. So be strong in the Lord and in the power of his might!

Acknowledgements

In my own spiritual warfare and in writing this book, I have found much help in the writings of Christian warriors from earlier centuries: William Gurnall, *The Christian in Complete Armor*; John Bunyan, *The Pilgrim's Progress* and *The Holy War;* Martyn Lloyd-Jones, *The Christian Warfare* and *The Christian Soldier;* and C. S. Lewis, *The Screwtape Letters.* Even when I do not quote from these sources, I owe them a great debt on nearly every page.

As a pastor of churches in Strathroy, Ontario, and Monee, Illinois, I learned and taught much of what I say in this book. At Back to God Ministries, I shared these things with an international audience, and I learned much from those who responded. As Provost of Christian Leaders Institute, I interact with students in many countries and gain insights from the battles they face. I rejoice at their eagerness to carry out the mission Jesus has given them, and I admire their Spirit-given courage to stand against evil.

Those who know me best and love me most—my family and, above all, the Lord of hosts—remain faithful to me despite my faults and defeats. Grace keeps me going. "I can do all things through Christ who strengthens me" (Philippians 4:13).

Christian Leaders Institute

Christian Leaders Institute provides free online ministry training worldwide. All people called by God, regardless of income, can become well trained leaders at no cost to them. Local mentors and pastors in many countries partner with CLI faculty in equipping thousands of new leaders.

David Feddes serves as Provost at Christian Leaders Institute. He oversees the curriculum and works with other professors to make sure that every course provides high quality ministry training. Many classes feature video presentations and writings by Dr. Feddes. CLI's goal is to raise up revival leaders with hearts full of Holy Spirit fire and minds formed by biblical truth.

If you are seeking no-cost, high quality ministry training, or if you would like to support CLI financially so that more leaders can be equipped for God's mission, please visit the CLI website: **www.christianleadersinstitute.org**